Books by Eric Hammel

76 Hours: The Invasion of Tarawa (with John E. Lane)
Chosin: Heroic Ordeal of the Korean War
The Root: The Marines in Beirut
Ace!: A Marine Night-Fighter Pilot in World War II
(with R. Bruce Porter)
Duel for the Golan (with Jerry Asher)
Guadalcanal: Starvation Island
Guadalcanal: The Carrier Battles
Guadalcanal: Decision at Sea
Munda Trail: The New Georgia Campaign
The Jolly Rogers (with Tom Blackburn)
Khe Sanh: Siege in the Clouds
First Across the Rhine (with David E. Pergrin)
Lima-6: A Marine Company Commander in Vietnam
(with Richard D. Camp)
Ambush Valley
Aces Against Japan
Aces Against Japan II
Aces Against Germany
Air War Europa: Chronology
Carrier Clash
Aces at War
Air War Pacific: Chronology
Aces in Combat
Bloody Tarawa
Marines at War
Carrier Strike
Pacific Warriors
Iwo Jima

IWO JIMA

ERIC HAMMEL

ZENITH PRESS

For the Fallen

First published in 2006 by Zenith Press, an imprint of MBI Publishing Company, 400 First Avenue North, Suite 300, Minneapolis, MN 55401 USA

Copyright © 2006, 2009 by Eric Hammel.

Hardcover edition published 2006. Softcover edition 2009.

Zenith Press titles are also available at discounts in bulk quantity for industrial or sales-promotional use. For details write to Special Sales Manager at MBI Publishing Company, 400 1st Avenue North, Minneapolis, MN 55401 USA.

To find out more about our books, visit us online at www.zenithpress.com.

ISBN-13: 978-0-7603-3733-2

Designer: Tom Heffron
Maps: Philip Schwartzberg, Meridian Mapping, Minneapolis

Photo credits:
On the cover: Official USMC photo
On the spine: Joe Rosenthal
On the back cover: Official USMC photo
On the frontispiece: Courtesy of the Marine Corps Acosiation
On the title page: Official USMC photo

The Library of Congress catalogued the hardcover edition of this title as follows:

Hammel, Eric M.
  Iwo Jima : portrait of a battle : United States Marines at war in the Pacific / Eric Hammel.
     p. cm.
  ISBN-13: 978-0-7603-2520-9 (hardbound w/ jacket)
  ISBN-10: 0-7603-2520-0 (hardbound w/ jacket)
  1. Iwo Jima, Battle of, Japan, 1945. I. Title.
  D767.99.I9H355 2006
  940.54'2528--dc22

                                                  2006015636

Printed in China

ERIC HAMMEL is a critically acclaimed military historian and author of nearly forty narrative and pictorial histories, including *Chosin: Heroic Ordeal of the Korean War*, *Marines in Hue City: A Portrait of Urban Combat, Tet 1968*, and *How America Saved the World: The Untold Story of U.S. Preparedness Between the World Wars*. He has written many titles on U.S. Marine operations in World War II, such as *Islands of Hell*, *Pacific Warriors*, and his *U.S. Marines in World War II* series—*Guadalcanal; New Georgia, Bougainville, and Cape Gloucester*; and *Tarawa and the Marshalls*.

Contents

Author's Note		6
Acknowledgments		7
Glossary		8
Maps		10
Chapter 1	Unsinkable Carrier—Impregnable Fortress	17
Chapter 2	Why Iwo Jima?	23
Chapter 3	Fortress Iwo	29
Chapter 4	Bombardment	39
Chapter 5	A Mighty Armada	47
Chapter 6	First to Fight	53
Chapter 7	Ship to Shore	59
Chapter 8	Beach Assault	69
Chapter 9	The Marines Have Landed	93
Chapter 10	Suribachi	105
Chapter 11	The Flag	117
Chapter 12	Up from the Beach	129
Chapter 13	All the Comforts	165
Chapter 14	Grinding Forward	173
Chapter 15	To Victory	199
Chapter 16	Justifying Iwo	243
Chapter 17	D + 60 Years	249
Bibliography		252
Index		254

Author's Note

I would like to start with a little story about me and "The Flag Raising at Iwo Jima"—The Photo—that I have no doubt has been repeated again and again in other places and times over the sixty years since The Photo's first publication. I have told this story to Joe Rosenthal.

In 1955 I was a student in Mrs. Lesches' fourth-grade class at Logan Elementary School in Philadelphia. I sat at the last desk in the second row, from which I could look straight out the door to the marble-wainscoted hallway. Opposite the door, and perfectly framed in it from my vantage point, was a colorized print of The Photo.

I was a good student, and Mrs. Lesches gave me a little slack; I could skylark out the door if she wasn't writing on the blackboard or speaking. This was never mentioned; I just picked up on it. So, for the year 1955, I looked out at The Photo every school day, and pretty soon I fell in love with it. I fell in love with my *idea* of it.

I grew up in the company of World War II vets. My own father was one. I knew an Iwo Jima vet. And I was raised in an especially patriotic time.

It stayed with me. In time I found that I could write—indeed, that I wanted to write. In more time I decided to write for my living. In pretty much no time I began to write military history—specifically Pacific War history. And so here I am, fifty years and thirty military history books later, relating a personal story that relates to a photo that relates that especially poignant and nearly magical long-ago moment on far-off Iwo Jima. The Photo wasn't the only thing that brought me to my vocation, and it wasn't the first. But I have no doubt that that school year of staring at it and imagining heroism crystallized all the other events of my youth that brought me here.

Eric Hammel
Northern California
Summer 2005

Acknowledgments

I wish to thank the indomitable staff at the Still Pictures branch of the National Archives and Records Administration, especially the ever-helpful, ever-patient, ever-cheerful Theresa M. Roy and Donna Larker. So too my many old friends on the staff of the Marine Corps University Archive at Quantico, Virginia.

Major Norman Hatch, who in my mind at least is the dean of Marine combat photographers, has always made himself available to offer advice. Norm formed and personally oversaw the 5th Marine Division photographic section for Iwo Jima, so to a large degree this book is a product of his dedication, ingenuity, and bravery.

I also particularly thank my friend and fellow author John R. Bruning Jr. for sharing his photos, his hands-on scanning assistance, his deep knowledge of digital scanning equipment and techniques, and his insights into best use of the National Archives' Still Pictures collection.

Many thanks, also, to my old and dear friend Master Chief Hospital Corpsman Mark Hacala, for providing photos of the Navy Hospital Corps Medal of Honor recipients; to Colonel Walt Ford of *Leatherneck* magazine for his never-failing kindness as well as some valuable instant research; to Jon Dodd and the Marine Corps Association art staff for digging out and scanning the frontispiece; and to Nancy Hoffman, also of *Leatherneck*, for photographing another in a running series of portraits of the aging author.

Glossary and Guide to Abbreviations

A6M Imperial Navy Mitsubishi single-engine Zero fighter

Amtrac Amphibian tractor

B-24 U.S. Army Air Forces Consolidated Liberator four-engine heavy bomber

B-25 U.S. Army Air Forces North American Mitchell twin-engine medium bomber; same as PBJ

B-29 U.S. Army Air Forces Boeing Superfortress four-engine very heavy bomber

BAR Browning Automatic Rifle

Bazooka 2.36-inch shoulder-fired antitank rocket launcher

C6N Imperial Navy Nakajima Myrt single-engine carrier reconnaissance plane

D-day Invasion day

D+1, etc. D-day plus 1 day, etc.

F4U U.S. Navy/Marine Corps Vought Corsair single-engine fighter

F6F U.S. Navy Grumman Hellcat single-engine fighter; F6F-5(N) variant employed by the U.S. Marine Corps as a night fighter

FM U.S. Navy General Motors Wildcat ground-support fighter

FMF Fleet Marine Force

FMFPac Fleet Marine Force, Pacific

G4M Imperial Navy Mitsubishi Betty twin-engine medium bomber

H-hour The time set for an invasion or assault to begin

LCI Landing craft, infantry

LCI(G) Landing craft, infantry, gunboat

LCI(R) Landing craft, infantry, rocket ship

LCM Landing craft, medium

LCT Landing craft, tank

LCVP Landing craft, vehicle, personnel

LSD Landing ship, dock

LSM Landing ship, medium

LST Landing ship, tank

LVT Landing vehicle, tracked; amphibious tractor

LVT(A) Landing vehicle, tracked, armored; amphibious tank

M3 Stuart light tank

M4 Sherman medium tank

M-1 U.S. Garand .30-caliber semiautomatic infantry rifle

MAG Marine Air Group

OA-10 U.S. Army Air Forces Consolidated twin-engine air-sea rescue plane; same as a PBY

OY U.S. Marine Corps light spotter plane from various manufacturers

P-38 U.S. Army Air Forces Lockheed Lightning twin-engine fighter

P-47 U.S. Army Air Forces Thunderbolt single-engine long-range fighter

P-51 U.S. Army Air Forces North American Mustang single-engine long-range fighter

P-61 U.S. Army Air Forces Northrop Black Widow twin-engine, two-place, radar-guided night fighter

PBJ U.S. Marine Corps North American twin-engine medium bomber/gunship; same as B-25

PBM U.S. Navy Martin Mariner twin-engine patrol bomber

PB4Y-2 U.S. Navy Consolidated Privateer four-engine patrol bomber; generally the same as B-24

PBY U.S. Navy Consolidated Catalina twin-engine patrol bomber

R4D U.S. Navy/Marine Douglas Dakota twin-engine transport; same as Army C-47 and civilian DC-3

SB2C U.S. Navy/Marine Corps Curtiss Helldiver single-engine scout-/dive-bomber

SBD U.S. Marine Corps Douglas Dauntless single-engine scout-/dive-bomber

TBM U.S. Navy/Marine Corps Grumman Avenger single-engine torpedo/light bomber

VAC V Amphibious Corps

VJ-Day Victory over Japan Day

VMB Marine Bombing Squadron

VMF Marine Fighting Squadron

VMF(N) Marine Night Fighting Squadron

VMO Marine Observation Squadron

VMR Marine Transport Squadron

VMSB Marine Scout-Bomber Squadron

VMTB Marine Torpedo Squadron

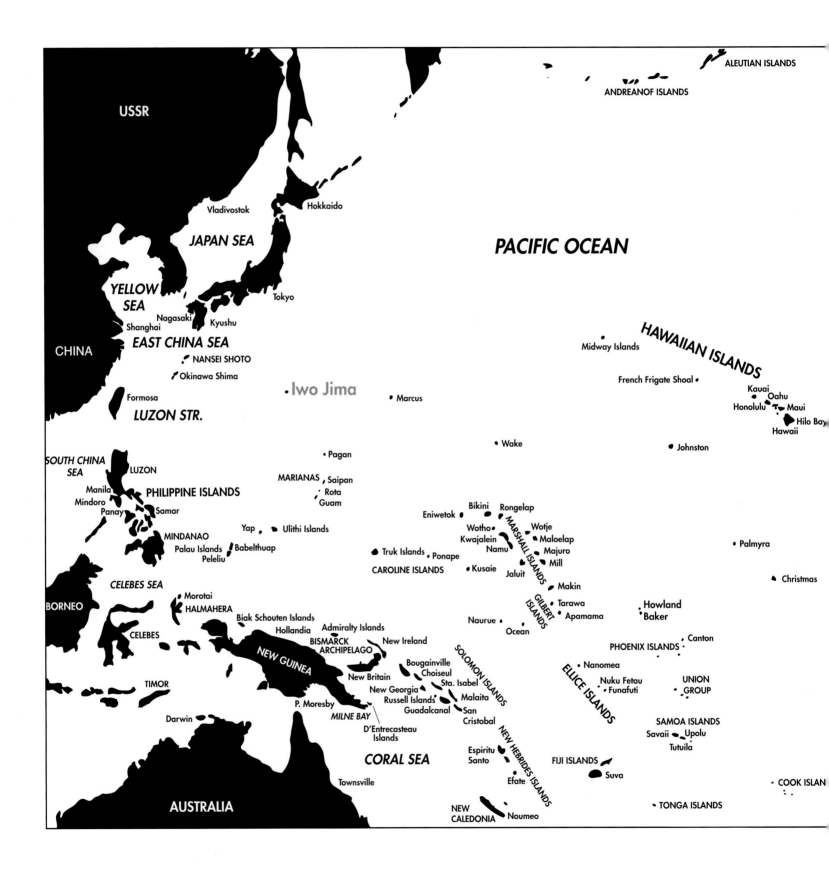

Maps

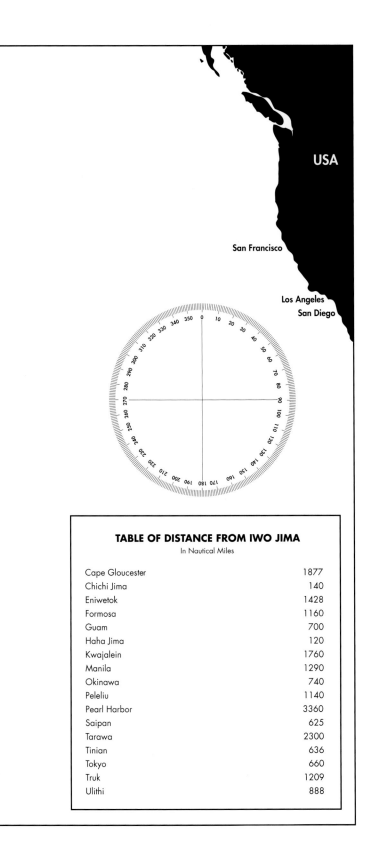

USA

San Francisco

Los Angeles
San Diego

TABLE OF DISTANCE FROM IWO JIMA
In Nautical Miles

Cape Gloucester	1877
Chichi Jima	140
Eniwetok	1428
Formosa	1160
Guam	700
Haha Jima	120
Kwajalein	1760
Manila	1290
Okinawa	740
Peleliu	1140
Pearl Harbor	3360
Saipan	625
Tarawa	2300
Tinian	636
Tokyo	660
Truk	1209
Ulithi	888

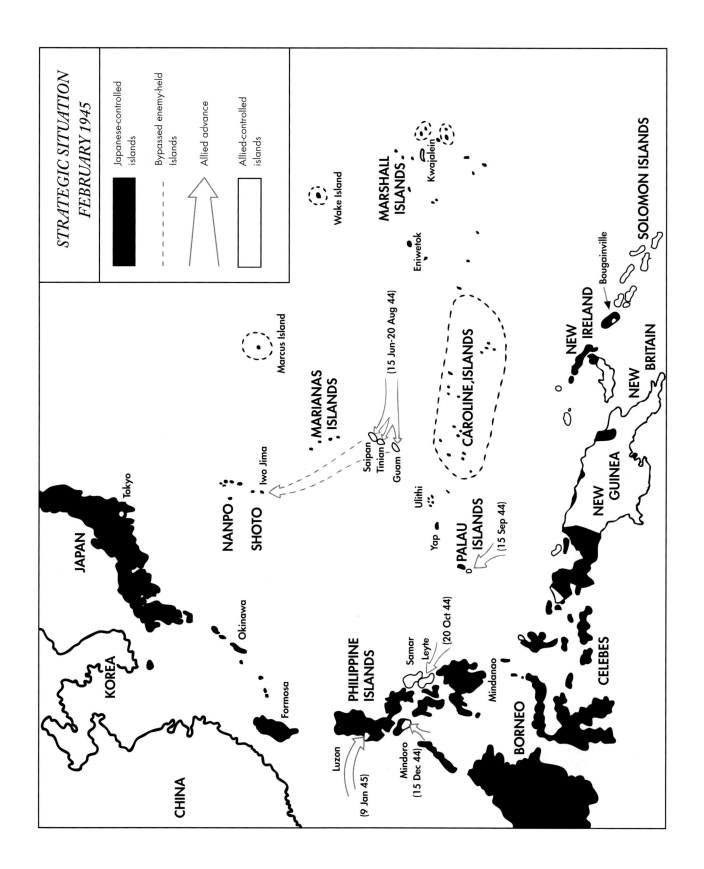

STRATEGIC SITUATION
FEBRUARY 1945

Japanese-controlled islands

Bypassed enemy-held Islands

Allied advance

Allied-controlled islands

CHINA

JAPAN

Tokyo

KOREA

Okinawa

Formosa

NANPO
SHOTO

Iwo Jima

MARIANAS
ISLANDS

Marcus Island

Saipan
Tinian
Guam

(15 Jun–20 Aug 44)

Ulithi

Yap

PALAU
ISLANDS

(15 Sep 44)

CAROLINE ISLANDS

PHILIPPINE
ISLANDS

Luzon

(9 Jan 45)

Mindoro
(15 Dec 44)

Samar
Leyte

(20 Oct 44)

Mindanao

BORNEO

CELEBES

NEW
GUINEA

NEW
IRELAND

NEW
BRITAIN

Bougainville

SOLOMON ISLANDS

MARSHALL
ISLANDS

Kwajalein

Eniwetok

Wake Island

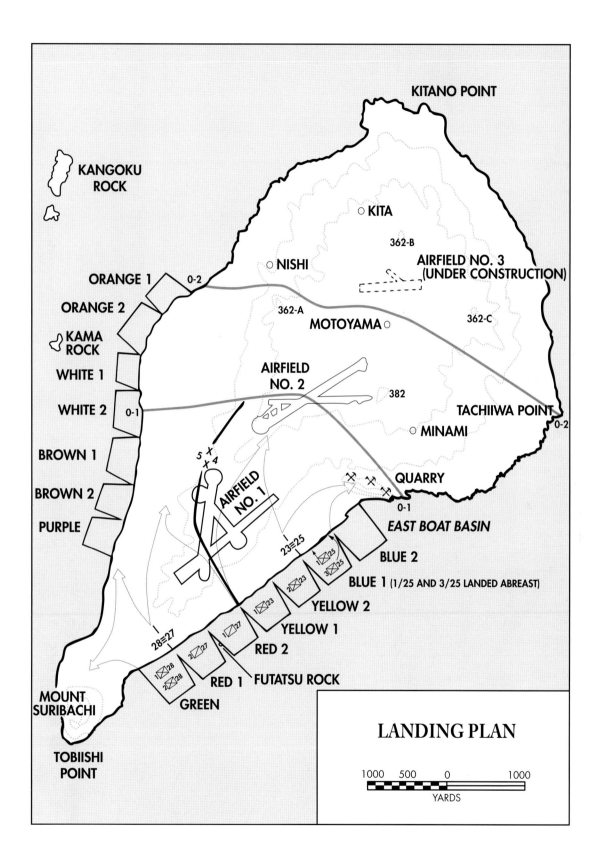

KITANO POINT

KANGOKU ROCK

○ KITA

362-B

○ NISHI

AIRFIELD NO. 3
(UNDER CONSTRUCTION)

ORANGE 1   0-2

ORANGE 2

362-A

KAMA ROCK

362-C

MOTOYAMA ○

WHITE 1

AIRFIELD NO. 2

WHITE 2   0-1

382

TACHIIWA POINT

0-2

○ MINAMI

BROWN 1

5 +
+ 4

+ +
+

BROWN 2

AIRFIELD NO. 1

QUARRY

0-1

PURPLE

EAST BOAT BASIN

23≡25

1 ⊠ 25
3 ⊠ 25

BLUE 2

2 ⊠ 23

BLUE 1 (1/25 AND 3/25 LANDED ABREAST)

1 ⊠ 23

YELLOW 2

YELLOW 1

1 ⊠ 27

RED 2

28≡27

2 ⊠ 27

FUTATSU ROCK

1 ⊠ 28
2 ⊠ 28

RED 1

MOUNT SURIBACHI

GREEN

LANDING PLAN

TOBIISHI POINT

1000   500   0   1000
YARDS

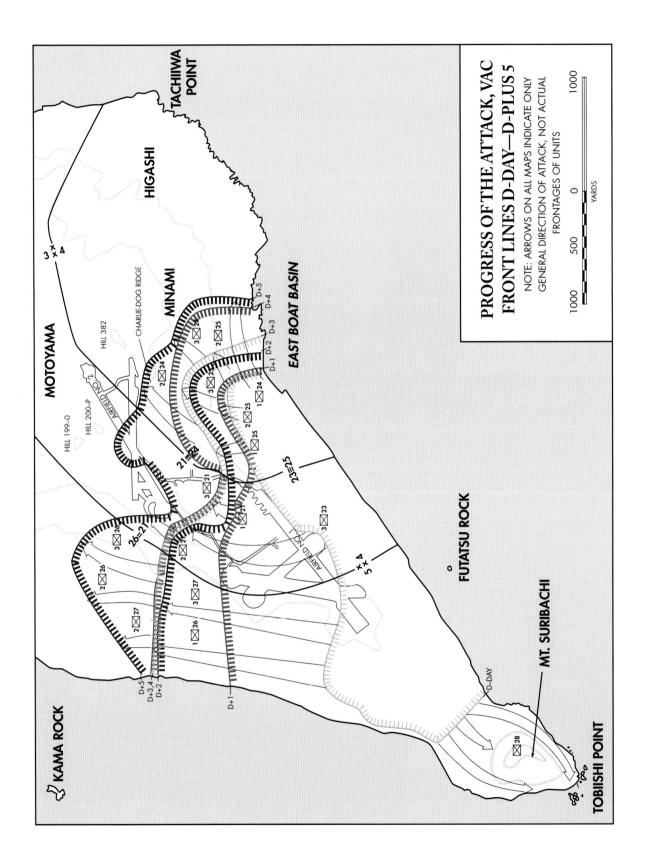

KAMA ROCK

MOTOYAMA

HILL 199-O

HILL 200-P

HILL 382

CHARLIE-DOG RIDGE

HIGASHI

TACHIIWA POINT

3 × 4
× ×

MINAMI

AIRFIELD NO. 2

3 | 24

2 | 24

1 | 24

3 | 24

2 | 25

1 | 25

2 | 25

D+1 D+2 D+3 D+4 D+5

EAST BOAT BASIN

21 ≡ 24

23 ≡ 25

3 | 21

1 | 21

3 | 26

26-2

2 | 26

2 | 26

2 | 27

1 | 26

3 | 27

AIRFIELD NO. 1

3 | 23

5 × 4
× ×

FUTATSU ROCK

D+5
D+3,4
D+2

D+1

MT. SURIBACHI

D-DAY

2 | 28

TOBIISHI POINT

PROGRESS OF THE ATTACK, VAC FRONT LINES D-DAY—D-PLUS 5

NOTE: ARROWS ON ALL MAPS INDICATE ONLY GENERAL DIRECTION OF ATTACK, NOT ACTUAL FRONTAGES OF UNITS

1000   500   0   1000

YARDS

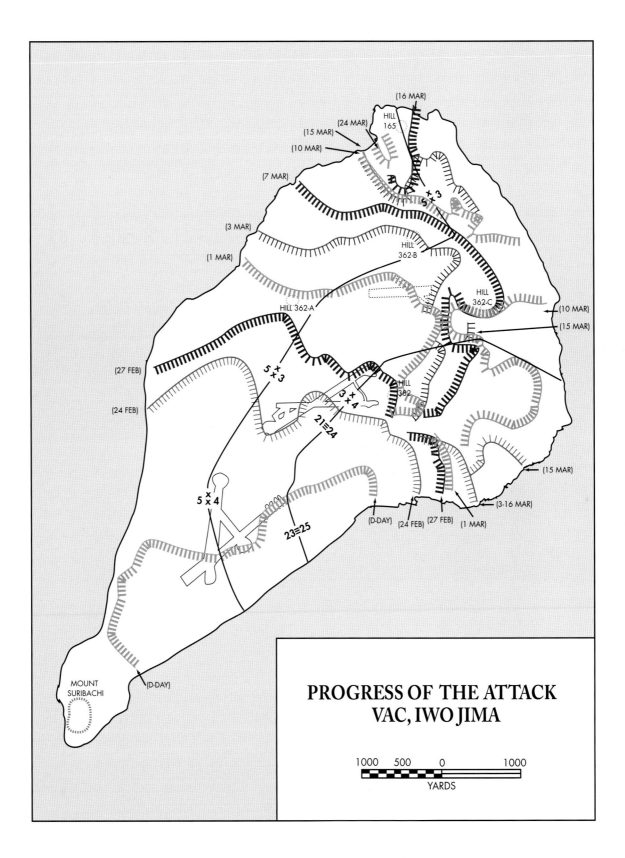

(16 MAR)

HILL 165

(24 MAR)

(15 MAR)

(10 MAR)

T

5 × 3

(7 MAR)

(3 MAR)

HILL 362-B

(1 MAR)

HILL 362-C

(10 MAR)

HILL 362-A

E

(15 MAR)

(27 FEB)

5 × 3

HILL 382

(24 FEB)

3 × 4

21 ≡ 24

(15 MAR)

(3-16 MAR)

5 × 4

(15 MAR)

23 ≡ 25

(D-DAY)

(24 FEB)

(27 FEB)

(1 MAR)

MOUNT SURIBACHI

(D-DAY)

PROGRESS OF THE ATTACK
VAC, IWO JIMA

1000   500   0   1000

YARDS

CHAPTER 1

Unsinkable Carrier—
Impregnable Fortress

The first Americans to see the Bonin and Volcano Island groups from the air were the crews of U.S. Navy fighters and bombers launched on June 15, 1944, from the fast carriers of Task Group 58.1 and Task Group 58.4. The Americans who struck the airfields at Iwo Jima, Haha Jima, and Chichi Jima were supporting the new invasion of the Mariana Islands, at Saipan, by cutting off the flow of aircraft from Japan to the Marianas via these bases. Despite heavy seas, the air groups from three fleet carriers and four light carriers mounted powerful afternoon strikes against the airfields, fuel supplies, and barracks. American fighter pilots from three F6F Hellcat squadrons knocked down forty A6M Zero fighters over Iwo Jima between 1445 and 1555 hours, and the Japanese shot down two TBM Avenger light bombers, two SB2C Helldiver dive-bombers, and three F6F fighters, killing all thirteen airmen aboard them.

This was an auspicious beginning to a deadly struggle that would ultimately claim the lives of nearly thirty thousand American and Japanese servicemen.

The carrier planes returned to all three islands the next day, June 16, and pretty much finished what they had begun on June 15. Two more F6Fs were lost with their pilots—one to antiaircraft fire and the other in an operational accident. The only Japanese plane lost in the air was a patrol bomber that was out looking for the carriers. In all, by the time the American carriers retired eastward toward the Marianas, two days of attacks had destroyed an estimated 41 Japanese aircraft in the air, 86 Japanese aircraft on the ground at Iwo Jima, and 21 seaplanes and floatplanes at their moorings at Chichi Jima. Ground facilities also were raked, and the bases were temporarily closed to large air movements.

Iwo Jima viewed from west to east. Mount Suribachi is to the right (south), Motoyama Airfield No. 1 is the first large bright patch to the north (left) of Suribachi, and Motoyama Airfield No. 2 is north of that. The future invasion beaches are on the eastern (far) side of the island, between Suribachi and Airfield No. 1. *National Archives & Records Administration*

A U.S. Navy Grumman F6F-5 Hellcat carrier fighter. *Official USN Photo*

U.S. Navy General Motors TBM torpedo/light carrier bombers. *Official USN Photo*

On June 23, Americans intercepted radio traffic indicating that an estimated one hundred Japanese warplanes were being concentrated on Iwo Jima, perhaps to attack the American fleet off Saipan. As a result, Task Group 58.1, then on its way to refit at Eniwetok, was diverted to mount new airfield-interdiction strikes against Iwo Jima. That very night, between midnight and 0100, Imperial Navy G4M Betty medium bombers flying out of Iwo dropped bombs over U.S. warships off Guam, but they caused no damage.

Beginning quite early on June 24, Task Group 58.1 aircraft were launched against airfields, fuel storage, and barracks on Iwo Jima. The Japanese countered by launching more than 140 fighters and bombers against the carriers. Of these, in a battle royal and several follow-on attacks over the sea, American F6F pilots claimed 116 confirmed victories, and antiaircraft gunners claimed a number over the task force. At sunset, Task Force 58.1 retired toward Eniwetok.

Task Group 58.1 returned to the Bonin and Volcano islands on July 3 in the company of Task Group 58.2. As surface warships bombarded the island bases for the first time, extremely effective air attacks were mounted through the afternoon, and carrier aircraft shot down a patrol bomber at sea and 49 Zero fighters over and around Iwo Jima. The next day—Independence Day—was more of the same; Iwo Jima and Chichi Jima were mercilessly bombed, strafed, and shelled; night-fighter pilots downed 7 float fighters over Chichi Jima before dawn; day fighters claimed 32 fighters, a patrol bomber, and a light bomber; and an observation plane was downed by a cruiser's antiaircraft battery.

A U.S. Navy Curtiss SB2C Helldiver carrier dive-bomber. *Official USN Photo*

A U.S. Navy carrier bomber's view of Chichi Jima harbor on July 4, 1944. *Official USN Photo*

Once the Japanese air defense was beaten down on July 4, this round of air attacks continued without aerial opposition against Chichi and Iwo on July 5 and 6, and warships stood close inshore to the defenseless bases for most of July 6 while the carriers departed toward the Marianas.

The next Americans to see Iwo Jima from the air were the crews of several U.S. Navy PB4Y four-engine heavy patrol bombers that flew up from their base on Saipan on July 14, 1944, to bomb Iwo, Chichi, and Haha. If the raid meant anything to the Japanese, it was that American land-based bombers could now reach the place from the Mariana Islands.

The PB4Ys returned on July 15 and 20, by which time the chastened Japanese had come to realize that the Bonin and Volcano islands were extremely vulnerable to invasion—

An attack by U.S. Navy carrier aircraft has caught many Japanese aircraft on the ground at Iwo Jima. The pillars of black smoke are from fires ignited by strafing runs against aircraft with fuel in their tanks. *National Archives & Records Administration*

A U.S. Navy cruiser fires her main guns pointblank against targets on Iwo Jima. This feat could be accomplished only after complete air supremacy had been attained over the island by U.S. Navy carrier aircraft. *Official USN Photo*

Taken after the invasion, this photo shows a landing ship destroyed and beached at Iwo Jima by U.S. Navy carrier aircraft on August 4, 1944. *Official USMC Photo*

The second landing ship, her bows blown off, was also beached on August 4, 1944. A freighter, also beached, is to the extreme right. *Official USMC Photo*

that the bases there were obviously being softened up by land-based bombers that could attack at will.

When the fast carriers of Task Group 58.1 and 58.3 returned on August 4, they for the first time interfered directly with Japanese efforts to build up the defenses. Few Japanese aircraft were encountered, but carrier bombers caught a mixed flotilla of five freighters, two large landing ships, a destroyer, and two destroyer-escorts as they upped anchor to flee from Iwo. The carrier planes destroyed all five freighters, the two landing ships, and the destroyer, and escorting U.S. Navy cruisers sank both destroyer-escorts. Attacks against the airfields on August 4, 5, and 6 stripped the bases of their aircraft, and surface bombardments flattened Iwo and Chichi. The entire force retired toward Eniwetok on the evening of August 6.

On August 10, U.S. Army Air Forces B-24 Liberator heavy bombers based on Saipan mounted their first mission against Iwo. They returned on August 14, 17, 23, and 25. On August 28, the Saipan-based B-24s mounted two missions against Iwo, one by day and another at night, then they returned by day on August 29.

U.S. Army Air Forces Consolidated B-24 Liberator heavy bombers during one of their many appearances over Iwo Jima. *Official Signal Corps Photo*

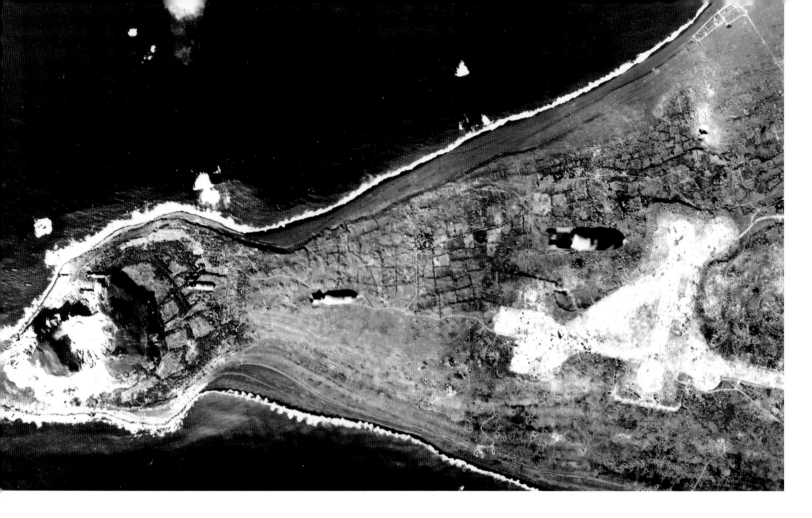

Bombs fall from a B-24 that is flying south to north over Mount Suribachi toward Motoyama Airfield No. 1. *Official Signal Corps Photo*

After some time off, during which the fast carrier task force was redesignated Task Force 38, the carriers of Task Group 38.4 returned to batter the Bonin and Volcano bases on September 1 and 2. Just one Imperial Navy reconnaissance bomber was encountered, and it was shot down at night by a night fighter. Attacks by B-24s resumed on September 3 and took place ten more times that month, by which time the carriers were totally absorbed in offensive operations in the Philippines. There were fourteen routine day and night missions by the Saipan-based B-24s, but one event was far from routine—indeed, it must have chilled the defenders when a Saipan-based Army Air Forces P-47 Thunderbolt fighter shot down a twin-engine Imperial Army fighter over Iwo at noon on October 21.

The routine nature of the bombing attacks combined with the ability of land-based fighters to reach Iwo certainly telegraphed the high probability that either an American amphibious assault was in the immediate offing, or that Iwo and nearby bases were to be bypassed and sealed by air power. The Japanese thought the former was more likely, and they redoubled their efforts to build up Iwo Jima's defenses, for an American invasion plan could only be interested in turning Iwo into an "unsinkable carrier" from which American aircraft could reach Japan itself. The Japanese had done the math as early as May 1944: a fighter that could reach Iwo from Saipan could reach Tokyo from Iwo. They knew well that the only way to forestall the conversion of Iwo into an unsinkable American carrier was first to turn it into an impregnable Japanese fortress.

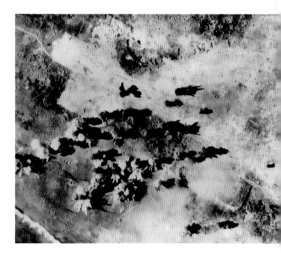

Bombs from a B-24 detonate on and near Motoyama Airfield No.1. *Official Signal Corps Photo*

CHAPTER 2

Why Iwo Jima?

Iwo Jima is one of the most isolated places on Earth. Waterless and barren, it is unsubtly hostile to human settlement. Today, as in days predating the opening of Japan to the world in the mid-nineteenth century, Iwo Jima rests at the very outer limit of the empire. Her only economic function has been the export of sulfur, a byproduct of the volcanic action that seethes barely beneath the island's mantle.

During the Pacific War Iwo Jima had only one function—as a watchpost against invasion of the inner empire. But her importance to Japan in late 1944 and early 1945 was also emotional; Iwo Jima was an integral component of the empire. Also, because she could support several large airfields—which nearby islands could not—she would naturally come under the eye of the American naval, air, and amphibious forces sweeping across the vast Pacific toward the Japanese home islands. The reasons for stoutly defending the otherwise useless and barren volcanic speck was first one of honor—for Iwo Jima was intrinsically Japanese; second, to deny the Americans the airfield sites for as long as possible; and third, to lay down the gauntlet, to communicate to the onrushing Americans that all of Japan would be as stoutly, as heroically, as unremittingly defended as was tiny, useless—but oh so Japanese—Iwo.

*   *   *

The blood bath at Iwo Jima in February and March 1945 owes itself entirely to the exigencies of the air war in the Pacific as a whole and specifically to the needs of the culminating phase of the strategic air offensive against the Japanese home islands.

Until mid-1944, when U.S. Marine and Army seized Japanese-held Saipan, Tinian, and Guam in the Mariana Islands, the Allied Pacific War strategy had been hobbled by the

Throughout 1944, as far as the Japanese could see, America's long-range air capability was bound up in the U.S. Navy's Fast Carrier Task Force. Each of the dozen or so wide-ranging fast carriers in the Fast Carrier Task Force could launch as many as a hundred light bombers and fighter-bombers against land targets, either in direct support of or far in advance of an island invasion. The ultimate goal of the U.S. Navy was to use fast-carrier air groups to throttle maritime trade within the shrinking empire as well as to attack military and industrial targets in Japan itself.
Official USN Photo

U.S. Army Air Forces Boeing B-29 Superfortress very heavy bombers of the XXI Bomber Command mounted the first of several "practice" missions against Iwo Jima, from Guam, on October 28, 1944. The B-29s in this photo are on one of those missions. *Official Signal Corps*

effective combat radius of land-based fighters. Simply put, to run an effective land-based bombing campaign against Japanese-held Pacific island bases, the U.S. Army Air Forces and Marine air commands in the Pacific had to provide numerous and effective fighter escorts. So, though bombers outranged fighters by a considerable margin, the advance up the Solomons chain, along the northern coast of New Guinea from late 1942 to mid-1944, across the central Pacific and through the Philippines had to take place at a pace of up to 300 miles per hop if the objective was to seize airfield sites from which Japanese bases farther out could be interdicted by fighter-escorted land-based bombers.

This linkage between the Allied Pacific offensive and the operational range of fighters (which was less than half their actual range) held up as a military law of nature until the unveiling of the U.S. Navy's fast carrier task force in late 1943. At that point, as new fleet carriers and light carriers began to arrive in the Pacific war zone at an average rate in excess of one per month, the 300-mile law could be bent somewhat if enough carriers could be shackled to a new objective long enough for ground troops to either seize an existing airfield that could be *quickly* rehabilitated or clear room for the *rapid* installation of a new airfield. As land-based fighters and fighter-bombers moved up to the new airfield, land-based bombers also could be brought forward, to support invasion troops ashore as well as to strike nearby bases that had been kept under the gun to that point by carrier air. At that point, the full weight of the fast carrier task

By late 1944, the U.S. Army Air Forces had perfected all three of its fighter escort types to achieve operational ranges in excess of the 650-mile trip to Iwo Jima from bases in the Marianas (as well as to Tokyo from Iwo Jima). Shown here are the VII Fighter Command's Consolidated P-47 Thunderbolt (left), Lockheed P-38 Lightning (center), and North American P-51 Mustang (right). Such ranges were achieved through a mix of large auxiliary fuel tanks, as shown on the P-51, coupled with strict fuel-conservation techniques developed earlier in the Pacific War by aviation pioneer Charles A. Lindbergh. *Official Signal Corps Photo*

force could be used to soften up new targets beyond the range of land-based fighters and, as the central Pacific campaign progressed, even beyond the range of land-based bombers. The addition of numerous escort carriers to the invasion fleets from late 1943 substantially enhanced the reach of the fast carriers, because escort-based air squadrons were trained and equipped to guard the invasion fleet *and* provide air support for forces ashore. Thus more fast carriers could move on to more distant assignments sooner than had been the case prior to the organization of flotillas of escort carriers.

The technological leap that nearly severed the link between the length of a new step forward and the operational range of land-based fighters was the appearance of U.S. Army Air Forces Boeing B-29 Superfortress very heavy bombers. These aerial giants, which were first employed out of forward bases in China, were built to fly at 32,000 feet—higher than most Japanese defensive fighters could reach—as well as to carry four tons of bombs out to ranges of 1,600 miles, and return. This was about 5,000 feet higher and 600 miles farther *in each direction* than the Consolidated B-24 Liberator heavy bomber.

The seizure of Saipan, Tinian, and Guam would place nearly all of Japan within range of a B-29-based bombing offensive as soon as highly reinforced, extra-long runways could be built on the three islands. The first B-29s reached Saipan on October 12, 1944;

The mainstay of the Army Air Forces' Pacific War bombing offensive through 1944 was the Consolidated B-24 Liberator four-engine heavy bomber, which could carry 5,000 pounds of bombs out to about a thousand miles at an altitude of 28,000 feet. The Pacific-based bomber commands deployed relatively few B-24 groups, but absent the B-29 program, experience in the European and Mediterranean theaters demonstrated that a massive B-24 bombing offensive against Japan, if supported by a massive fighter-escort program, could have achieved devastating results if mounted from bases as far away as Iwo Jima. The cost would have been high, but the outcome was assured. *Official Signal Corps Photos*

Shown here is a Japanese freighter under attack off the coast of Korea by a single U.S. Navy PB4Y long-range patrol bomber (a B-24 variant). Taken late in the war, it demonstrates the result the Japanese feared most from the seizure of an island air base as close as Iwo—the ability of American land-based aircraft to assault coastal shipping between the home islands and to and from offshore possessions, especially the Netherlands East Indies, China, and Korea. If Allied land-based bombers and long-range fighter-bombers could be loosed upon the empire's internal waterways, ports, and bases, there would have been no safe havens, no respite whatsoever for the Imperial Navy or the trade upon which Japan absolutely depended. *Official USN Photo*

several groups ran a training mission against Japanese-held Truk on October 28; and six of seventeen B-29s dispatched from Guam attacked Iwo Jima on November 8 (at a range of nearly 650 miles), the first of several winter "training" missions to Iwo. Finally, on the night of February 4, 1945, sixty-nine Marianas-based XXI Bomber Command B-29s flew all the way to Kobe, while thirty other B-29s that failed to find the city bombed targets of opportunity and last resort. Two B-29s failed to return.

Other than as a practice target in the run-up to the February 4 attack, Iwo Jima as yet had no direct role in the B-29 strategy, but it stood at the apex of a shallow equilateral triangle, roughly half the distance between the Marianas and central Japan.

By early 1945, all three of the Army Air Forces' long-range, high-altitude fighter types... P-38 Lightnings, P-47 Thunderbolts, and P-51 Mustangs—had been refined to the point at which their operational range was more than the distance between Iwo Jima and Tokyo. Iwo Jima, as an air base, stood at an optimum point for emergency landings by damaged or malfunctioning B-29s on their way to or from Japan and the Marianas—*and* as the extreme launch point for long-range fighters that could provide day escort for B-29s over Japanese cities and industrial zones.

In a nutshell, Iwo Jima or a neighboring island in the Volcano or Bonin island groups was the most suitable site for an emergency airfield and advance fighter base in support of the upcoming strategic bombing offensive against the Japanese homeland. All of the calculus by which invasion targets were selected that late in the Pacific War ground out inexorable results to all of the mathematical inputs bound up in distances and even in the tradeoffs in lives laid on the line to seize the bases as opposed to lives saved by having airfields available

Here, in another photo taken late in the war, Army Air Forces North American B-25 Mitchell twin-engine bombers based in the Philippines attack an Imperial Navy frigate off the Indochina coast. By the spring of 1945, Marine B-25 gunships (dubbed PBJs) based on Iwo wreaked exactly this sort of havoc upon shipping in southern Japan proper. *Official Signal Corps Photo*

Army Air Forces Northrop P-61 Black Widow night fighters, armed with 20mm cannon and .50-caliber machine guns, were scheduled for deployment to Iwo once the air bases there were seized and rehabilitated. By early 1945, radar-guided P-61s were being routinely employed over northern Italy as night hecklers. Though never used in that role in the Pacific, Iwo-based P-61s equipped with auxiliary fuel tanks could easily have been employed as night hecklers all the way into central Japan. *Official Signal Corps Photo*

for emergency landings, not to mention fighter escorts that could reach central Japan. Indeed, twin-engine North American B-25 medium bombers (designated PBJ by the Marine Corps) would be able to attack Japanese shipping and shore targets in southern Japan from Iwo Jima, a minor but nonetheless interesting bonus.

There were other islands near Iwo Jima that would have been fine as advance support bases that late in the war, but Iwo Jima was the only one that could support the very long runways required by the B-29s. The Japanese did not realize this, because they knew very little about the B-29 program, but they very well comprehended the offensive value Iwo Jima would have if the largest, longest-ranged American heavy bomber of the last phase of the Pacific War would have remained the B-24, because B-24s based at or staging through Iwo Jima from the Marianas would have complete access to all of Japan. Moreover, they knew that Iwo-based, state-of-the-art fighter escorts would be able to range over all of the southern two-thirds of Japan.

Even without factoring in the B-29 program, the Japanese knew that Iwo Jima was a highly likely target of American strategic planners, so they decided to defend it as heavily as their reeling war industry and burgeoning manpower needs could support. The fact that Iwo Jima stood at the extremity of the pre-war Japanese Empire added honor—and thus intractable stubbornness—to the mix of defensive priorities in a way American invasion forces had not yet experienced in the Pacific.

By mid-1944, U.S. Navy lifeguard submarines were routinely deployed off Japanese-held islands under attack by American land- and carrier-based aircraft. This use of vulnerable submarines can be taken as a sign of disdain toward Japan's ability to defend herself, but it also demonstrates the sheer wealth of the oncoming American tidal wave. By 1944, the U.S. Navy had on its rolls enough submarines to throttle Japan's maritime trade as well as to look out for individual pilots and aircrewmen forced to set down in a vast ocean. This Army Air Forces fighter pilot ditched on his way back from Japan to Iwo Jima in mid-1945. *Official USN Photo*

CHAPTER 3

Fortress Iwo

The Japanese architect of the Iwo Jima battle plan was Lieutenant General Tadamichi Kuribayashi, who was handed his assignment directly by the prime minister, General Hideki Tojo, in late May 1944—a month ahead of the first American carrier strikes. Even then the Japanese strategists knew that their defense of Iwo would be a rear-guard battle fought to gain time for the defense of the home islands to take shape.

Kuribayashi was a well-traveled fifty-four-year-old who had served two of his thirty years in uniform in the United States. He knew what he was up against in terms of industrial might and described Americans thusly: "the people are energetic and versatile. One must never underestimate the American's fighting ability."

The new island commander, who reached Iwo between June 8 and 10, 1944, experienced American energy once again through all of the summer's air attacks, during which the island's air-defense contingent was virtually annihilated. Certain the attacks presaged an imminent direct invasion, Kuribayashi and the rest of the island's too-few defenders awaited a similar annihilation. They were flabbergasted when it failed to materialize.

As Kuribayashi settled in to his apparently final service to his emperor, his thinking departed radically from—but built upon—that of colleagues all across the wide Pacific. Rather than bank everything on a beachside defense, Kuribayashi ordered his troops to construct interlocking defenses through the island's rough interior. And rather than hold troops back for a mobile defense in the open, he decreed that nearly every defender remain in cover until blown up or pried out at the point of bayonets. And the entire island would be covered beneath interlocking fans of artillery, mortars, and rockets. The Japanese defensive tactics

With no natural water source except for rain, and few natural water catchments, a top construction priority as Iwo Jima's defensive garrison rose in numbers was the maintenance of an adequate water supply. Men working in harrowing conditions—within the hot mantle of a quiescent volcano—required yet more water than might have been needed by troops at hard labor in more hospitable surroundings. Seen here is a small reservoir hewn directly into a sandstone crevice near the eastern side of the island. *Official USMC Photo*

A row of five cisterns constructed with steel-reinforced concrete near the center of the island. *Official USMC Photo*

The Japanese began their effort toward a planned 17-mile cave system by exploiting natural cave formations in the sandstone deposits found throughout Iwo Jima. Because of the lay of the land here, this particular cluster of caves in central Iwo Jima could not be reached by bombs, naval gunfire, or land-based artillery. *Official USMC Photo*

American planners had come to count on for quick victory on Pacific islands would not be used; Kuribayashi's brief to gain time for the homeland defense dictated a long, bloody battle of attrition.

As the troops already on Iwo dug in, Kuribayashi's nominal and newly stood up 109th Infantry Division began to be filled out with reinforcements. The 5,000-man 2d Independent Mixed Brigade was transferred from Chichi Jima, and the 2,700-man 145th Infantry Regiment, which had been earmarked for Saipan before that island was invaded in June 1944, also was sent to Iwo. Next to arrive was a 1,200-man naval construction battalion, followed by 2,200 naval infantry troops and aviation ground personnel. A mixed bag

This is the entrance to a concrete ammunition storage bunker. Note that the stone-lined concrete entry is below the level of the ground and well masked from bursting artillery rounds. *Official USMC Photo*

This concrete-faced tunnel entrance on the eastern side of Iwo Jima leads to a complex of hospital and communications bunkers deep beneath the surface. Note that there is little scarring from bullets and none from artillery fire. The stones piled atop the entrance serve both to camouflage against aerial observation and, together with stones lining the entry trench, provide further protection against bombs and artillery fire. *Official USMC Photo*

This tunnel, on the east side of the island just north of the invasion beaches, is hewn through stone. It is typical of miles of tunnel systems running throughout the island. *Official USMC Photo*

This elaborate and well-built trenchwork services a rocket-launcher emplacement in northeastern Iwo Jima. It consists of a stone-lined trench covered over with logs and no doubt well camouflaged above. *Official USMC Photo*

The thick overhead cover of the three pillboxes shown here is typical of pillboxes throughout Iwo Jima. Assigned just one machine gun each with a relatively restricted field of fire (note the fan of dirt to the sides of the embrasures of all three), these pillboxes are constructed of steel-reinforced concrete. Despite a direct hit by a fairly large-caliber shell, bomb, or rocket the second pillbox (situated above the invasion beaches) remained in action until taken out by direct assault. Likewise the third pillbox, which also overlooks the invasion beaches. A very near miss by a large-caliber shell, seen to the right of the embrasure in the third photo, merely scarred the concrete and at most stunned the gun crew. *Official USMC Photos*

of artillery units and five antitank battalions came next, but thereafter U.S. Navy submarines clung to the sea lanes to Iwo, sinking many supply ships through the late summer and autumn. One spread of torpedoes took to the bottom most of the barbed wire to be allotted to Iwo, and all twenty-eight of the vehicles of the tank regiment assigned to Iwo also were lost with their transport. Nevertheless, twenty-two tanks were replaced in due course (every one of them was dug in to a static emplacement) and the artillery strength rose to 361 artillery pieces rated at 75mm or over, 94 dual-purpose antiaircraft guns rated 75mm or over, 33 dual-purpose naval guns rated 80mm or over, 12 320mm spigot mortars, 65 150mm and 81mm mortars, more than 200 20mm and 25mm antiaircraft guns, 69 47mm and 37mm antitank guns, and an array of 70 rocket weapons with warheads rated between 200 pounds and 550 pounds. Lighter weapons included every type offered to ground-combat units of the Imperial Army and Imperial Navy, from infantry rifles and

This precast concrete emplacement looks huge and formidable in the first photo, but it is revealed as a rather claustrophobic one- or two-man position barely large enough to deploy a light machine gun. The crew of this position had barely enough room to crawl into the entry and stand up. One nevertheless has to admire the ingenuity and attention to detail, not to mention the workmanship, behind an emplacement like this. Note, in the second photo, the wide, flat field of fire dominated by this one emplacement as well as the care devoted to protecting the entry with stone blocks.
Official USMC Photos

Note, once again, the hard work, resources, attention to detail, and workmanship behind this little one-man fighting position overlooking one of the invasion beaches. *Official USMC Photo*

This dual antiaircraft gun mount doubled as antiboat defense in its position overlooking a beach not actually used by the invasion forces. Easily seen from the air because antiaircraft guns require a clear overhead view, it was no doubt eliminated before the invasion by aerial bombs or rockets, or perhaps by naval gunfire directed by an aerial spotter. *Official USMC Photo*

This is an open heavy machine gun emplacement, simple in concept: there is a packed-earth firing step; a prefabricated concrete embrasure; stacked, fitted stone blocks for both frontal and side protection as well as for camouflage; and a good field of fire across a valley or wide gully. *Official USMC Photo*

This dual-purpose 5-inch gun, in north-central Iwo Jima with a clear vista down the long axis of the island, has no doubt gone down fighting. Note the spent shell casing lying directly beneath the breech. This position, set on a low hummock, is constructed from masonry reinforced on the outside by earth. *Official USMC Photo*

This apparently unscathed 5-inch dual-purpose naval-type gun is sited high on the northeastern quadrant of Mount Suribachi to provide, first, antiaircraft defense, then antiship and antiboat defense, and finally antipersonnel defense. In its antiaircraft role it required overhead vistas all around, but it was stoutly protected from all but a direct hit by a ring of earth-filled fuel drums set in above and below ground level. Note that ready ammunition is neatly stacked in a bin seen on the left side of the photo above. *Official USMC Photos*

This 81mm mortar position clearly demonstrates the remarkable lengths to which Iwo Jima's defenders would go to develop the perfect defense even while knowing that no one on Earth believed the defenders had even a remote chance of overcoming the invaders. The single medium mortar is set in a masonry position in which the stone blocks have been cemented in place. The ammunition storage and crew shelter, accessed via a masonry-baffled entryway, is similarly built beneath a mantle of earth camouflaged with living plants and sculpted to be invisible from the air. For all that, because of the nature of mortars, the whole working part of this lavish emplacement is open to the sky and thus vulnerable to aerial observation followed by every kind of explosive that can be brought to bear. The man-hours that went into this one position must have been astronomical beside the benefit the single gun provided to the defense. *Official USMC Photo*

This Type 97 medium tank, one of 22 Japanese tanks on Iwo Jima, was, like all its mates, intentionally immobilized to act as a steel pillbox. This particular tank looks down from Hill 382 in central Iwo Jima. *Official USMC Photo*

light, medium, and heavy machine guns to the small 70mm field guns assigned to infantry battalions. There were gaps in weapons rations caused by American action against the sea lanes, but, one way or another, every defensive unit achieved more or less its assigned fighting capability.

Fully 25 percent of the troops who reached Iwo were assigned to tunneling operations. The tunnels were designed for two purposes—deep protection against air attack and interior lines of communication that would be maximally difficult for invaders to sever. Every type of defensive emplacement or bunker imaginable was built, from one-man spider holes to huge underground living and command bunkers. Many individual and crewed light-weapon emplacements were lined with stone or even constructed from precast concrete.

In the end, even though General Kuribayashi's defensive arrangements were not completed, Iwo Jima was in a class by itself, the ultimate expression of death and mayhem for the sake of death and mayhem to be found in the annals of the Pacific War. Improving exponentially on a "defend and die" concept first encountered by U.S. Army troops on Biak, in the Schouten Islands off New Guinea, and then by Marines at Peleliu, the island commander insisted upon the construction of hundreds of bunkers, pillboxes, blockhouses, and other fighting positions as well as multistory underground command centers and underground barracks—some as deep at 75 feet, and all interconnected by D-day by 11 of a planned 17 *miles* of underground passageways.

Reinforcements continued to arrive until early February 1945. Thus an estimated 23,000 Imperial troops, many of them veterans, were on hand to defend Iwo. The hundreds of mortars, artillery pieces, and rockets emplaced throughout the internal defensive

This is one of many steel-reinforced concrete personnel shelters spotted throughout the island. Both entryways are shielded by earthen barriers and the shelter is camouflaged overhead by earth and weeds. These shelters could accommodate about twenty troops. Marines found them handy to have around throughout the campaign, and many were used by both sides as ad hoc aid stations and command posts. *Official USMC Photo*

A one-man rifle pit or spider hole like this one could be the bane of an attacking force of even considerable size. If the occupant had good overhead cover that could be pushed off and pulled on, it might take much time and a number of lives to locate him as he fired at oncoming troops or even attackers who had already passed. With good communications, a defender who had been bypassed could direct fire into the American rear. Once again, consider the thought, effort, and workmanship invested in this single one-man fighting position. It is quite remarkable. *Official USMC Photo*

This machine-gun emplacement is more complicated than it appears here at first glance. Camouflaged and reinforced by natural materials—logs, stones, and earth—it is actually constructed in the main from stone blocks It appears from the displaced rubble used for overhead cover that the position runs back at least several yards, perhaps as far back as the reverse slope of the hummock into which it has been built. No doubt there is a covered, blastproof, and camouflaged entry back there. A pillbox like this is impossible to detect except from very close in. *Official USMC Photo*

sectors were painstakingly preregistered to cover virtually every square yard of the island. Nearly all the defenders had been bonded into a brotherhood born of rugged training (70 percent of their waking time) and the extreme difficulties encountered during the building of bunkers and passageways underground in extreme heat laced with sulfurous fumes. Beyond that, all the defenders took a solemn oath to fight to the death, to give no ground for any reason short of death. All questions of counterattacking the invaders were quelled when Kuribayashi sacked eighteen senior officers who openly disagreed with his static-defense strategy; except for designated roving assault detachments, the defenders would man their positions unto death.

There was no dead ground on Iwo Jima, not one spot that could be employed as cover with any certainty whatsoever that it was in fact cover. The only way to find dead ground was to kill for it.

CHAPTER 4

Bombardment

While the summer and early autumn air offensive against the Iwo Jima airfields was serious and pervasive, the effort to support the actual invasion of Iwo Jima, which was set for February 19, 1945, did not begin in earnest until November 1, 1944. On that date, several U.S. Navy PB4Y photographic-reconnaissance bombers were mixed in with the twelve Guam-based B-24s that attacked Iwo, Chichi, and Haha. Eight other B-24s attacked shipping in the area.

The significance of the first aerial photographic mission over Iwo was that it created an inventory of specific targets—other than the obvious airfields—that would be attacked systematically before the invasion. It also was the first attempt to provide Marine and navy invasion planners with oblique-angle photos from which, among many other things, specific landing beaches could be deduced.

Routine bombing attacks were mounted against one or another island in the Volcano and Bonin groups on seven of the first eight days of November. On November 9, the B-24s were charged with attacking antiaircraft emplacements on Haha and shipping wherever it could be found in the Bonins. These B-24s also strafed Iwo Jima on their return flight.

The specific targeting of antiaircraft emplacements signaled the beginning of the last phase by the Americans to achieve total aerial supremacy for the final run-up to the invasion. If aerial supremacy could be achieved—if American air power literally ruled the sky over the invasion objective—the orderly progression of a state-of-the-art storm landing and the subsequent land campaign was assured.

A Marine Bombing Squadron (VMB) 612 PBJ night heckler on a test flight. Note the radar installation on the nose, the matte black finish, and the scarcity of markings. The VMB-612 PBJs were unique in that they had these features as well as wing-loaded bombs and rockets. A rocket can be seen on the near wing. *Official USMC Photo*

Bombs and rockets are being loaded and readied for a night-heckler mission by this VMB-612 PBJ. The night missions were designed to keep the Japanese awake and on edge, a tactic learned from the Japanese as early as Guadalcanal in mid-1942. The night PBJs also attacked shipping targets, another of the squadron's unique specialties. *Official USMC Photo*

And so it went through the remainder of November: an attack roughly one of every two days continued to beat down the defenses and infrastructure throughout the Bonin and Volcano islands. Photoreconnaissance missions were run on November 13, 25, and 30. Bombers and photoreconnaissance aircraft returned on December 3.

As the bombing campaign in the Bonin and Volcano islands progressed, XXI Bomber Command B-29s conducted missions to Japan. These attacks were infrequent and small—the B-29s were testing their doctrine and learning the ropes—but it was obvious from the outset that damaged and malfunctioning Superforts really did need a halfway point at which they could save themselves from ditching in the immense Pacific. Lifeguard submarines seeded along the flight path between the Marianas bases and Japanese targets did not suffice. Moreover, fighter escorts were needed over the targets.

* * *

At 1030 hours on December 5, VII Fighter Command P-47s based at Saipan were vectored out to intercept a single bogey (unidentified aircraft) approaching from the northwest. The bogey, which was easily shot down, was a Nakajima C6N single-engine carrier-type reconnaissance plane. It was a virtual certainty that the C6N had *not* been launched from a carrier; the intelligence folks thought it probably was based at Iwo Jima. There was no chance to get planes over Iwo on December 6.

At 0404 hours on December 7, several Iwo-based Imperial Navy Mitsubishi G4M medium bombers suddenly strafed airfields in Saipan, and at 1435 hours thirteen Iwo-based G4Ms bombed the same airfields. Six of these G4Ms were shot down by antiaircraft fire, but they and their mates totally destroyed three B-29s, severely damaged three, and lightly damaged twenty others.

These raids were a dangerous affront to the Army Air Forces; they needed to be forestalled at the source. They also signaled

Scorched earth. This moonscape is a view of the dispersal and servicing areas of one of Iwo's two active airfields. A close look will reveal numerous aircraft (presumably damaged or destroyed) as well as an array of near-circular antiaircraft emplacements. Bomb craters are visible throughout. *National Archives & Records Administration*

This is a phony bunker with a phony gun barrel. It was meant to attract bombs, rockets, and naval gunfire away from real emplacements. *Official USMC Photo*

A U.S. Navy pilot's view of an Iwo Jima construction site just before he dropped his bomb or fired into the site with rockets or machine guns. A close look at the left side of the photo, above the surf line, will reveal seven or eight Japanese fleeing the scene. *Official USN Photo*

that the Japanese still had fight left in them and that all the aerial efforts over Iwo so far had had no lasting consequences.

Retribution was swift and overwhelming. On December 8—the day after the humiliating Saipan raids—61 of 82 B-29s dispatched from the Marianas joined 102 VII Bomber Command B-24s in an effort to destroy Iwo's capacity to host airplanes. The day's action over Iwo began at 0945 with a low-level sweep by 28 VII Fighter Command P-38 twin-engine fighters. The bombers then dropped more than 800 tons of bombs, and then a U.S. Navy surface task force stood in to pummel the island mercilessly. The lone Zero fighter that rose to the defense was easily swatted down.

The December 8 attacks heralded the start of the final phase of preinvasion attacks against Iwo Jima. Thereafter, for 73 consecutive days, including days on which only night-harassment missions were undertaken, the island's defenses and infrastructure were pounded from the air, mainly by B-24s. Along the way, the Marine Corps' VMB-612, in radar-guided PBJ gunships, mounted night-heckler bombing and strafing missions to Iwo. Also during this period, U.S. Navy surface battle forces, B-29s, and VII Fighter Command fighter-bombers returned to Iwo on an increasingly busy schedule.

This exciting view was taken from a U.S. Navy carrier plane as it came down very low to strafe a truck being loaded with fuel drums. Three or four Japanese troops dressed in rain slickers have been caught by surprise. *Official USN Photo*

Iwo's last gasp as an air base came on Christmas evening despite a sound pummeling on December 24 by 23 B-29s, 50 B-24s, and 17 P-38s, and a Christmas Day attack by a dozen B-24s. In what proved to be a final act of defiance, a stream of 25 Iwo-based G4Ms bombed and strafed parked B-29s on Saipan between 2000 and 2300 hours, destroying two and severely damaging another. Six of the G4Ms were shot down by VII Fighter Command night fighters.

Iwo Jima was struck next on December 27 by surface warships, 48 B-24s, and P-38 strafers. An Imperial Army twin-engine fighter was shot down by a P-38. Small follow-on attacks were mounted on December 29, 30, and 31. And during the night of December 31–January 1, in the strongest showing of its type so far in an almost-nightly campaign, ten VII Bomber Command B-24s streamed over Iwo to bomb and strafe during a six-hour period.

At 0450 hours on January 1, 1945, a VII Fighter Command night fighter shot down a G4M over Tinian. The bomber could have come only

During the final run-up to the invasion, a U.S. Navy destroyer, beautifully decked out in camouflage paint, fires her forward and after 5-inch guns directly at a target on the beach visible to her gun crews. This warship is close inshore and appears to be making her way very slowly along the beach. *Official USN Photo*

The cruiser in the foreground (and certainly the warships closer in) has her main guns level so she can fire directly on beachside targets ashore. The beaches are shrouded in smoke from many shell bursts, but there is no evidence of answering fire. *Official USN Photo*

from Iwo. On January 2, between 0450 and 1255 hours, Army Air Forces fighters downed over Tinian a G4M, an Imperial Navy land-based patrol bomber, and a C6N.

Routine day and night missions were run against Iwo every day between January 1 and January 4. On January 5, in a new mission for VII Bomber Command, B-24s served as spotter planes as U.S. Navy surface warships and aircraft from Task Force 38 attacked Iwo, Haha, and Chichi. Taking part in attacks against these targets for the first time were Marine F4U Corsairs from VMF-124 and VMF-213, which were newly embarked in the fleet carrier USS *Essex*. Also during that day, U.S. Navy PB4Y photoreconnaissance bombers kicked off an effort to complete their coverage of the defenses on Iwo. One Zero rose to defend Iwo, and it was shot down by a P-38 strafer.

Routine attacks resumed through January 23. Lone Japanese snoopers were intercepted and shot down over the Marianas on January 14 and 15. On January 24, 53 XXI Bomber Command B-29s attacked the island's defenses. Also on that day, B-24s once again served as spotter planes for bombardment vessels. Routine day and night missions were run every day for the rest of the month.

On January 31, the Iwo Jima Air Support Plan went into effect, so on February 1—with eighteen days to D-day—VII Bomber Command raised the average number of B-24s dispatched on a routine day mission against Iwo from about ten to about twenty; B-24 night bombers remained at about ten. On February 3—two weeks ahead of D-day—P-38s escorting photoreconnaissance PB4Ys strafed the defenses at low level then routine missions resumed.

On February 9, photo analysts concluded that the daily bombing attacks commencing on December 8 had *not* been effective in halting the construction of numerous new defensive emplacements, nor even the installation of many new artillery pieces. Nevertheless, VII Bomber Command chugged along with twenty-odd bombers on February 10 and 11, but on February 12—only a week before D-day—21 XXI Bomber Command B-29s, using radar guidance, added 84 tons of bombs to the usual dose when they went after gun emplacements on Mount Suribachi from high altitude. It was a nice gesture and an interesting experiment, but the results were negligible. There were routine bombing attacks on February 13, 14, and 15.

* * *

The intensity of the preinvasion bombardment program climbed precipitously on February 16. In the first place, the Fast Carrier Task Force—once again Task Force 58—interposed itself between Iwo Jima and airfields on Honshu from which Iwo Jima might receive support or from which a last-minute kamikaze surge against the invasion fleet might be mounted (as it had been in the Philippines just a few months earlier). At the end of the day—after striking many strategic targets that had nothing to do with aircraft interdiction—Task Force 58 retired toward Iwo Jima.

Closer in on February 16, nine escort carriers organized as the Amphibious Support Carrier Group (Task Group 52.2) arrived off Iwo in bad weather and rough seas to begin softening up the defenses for real. The airmen aboard the escort carriers were trained specifically for their mission and went about it in a spirited manner. For February 16, however, high spirits were trumped by miserable weather. Planned strikes by carrier-based FM fighter-bombers and TBM light bombers were scrubbed.

Arriving with the escorts was a powerful armada of surface warships, including "old" pre-war battleships that had been relegated to a gunfire-support role because they could not keep pace with the fast carriers. The warships and 42 VII Bomber Command B-24s were able to undertake their assigned bombardment missions.

The weather cleared on February 17, and the FMs aboard the escort carriers completed 226 effective combat sorties against Iwo's airfield defenses. Many napalm bombs were dropped by the FMs to burn off cover, but the results were disappointing because there wasn't all that much vegetation to burn off. The intense naval bombardment continued apace, and 42 B-24s attacked from only 5,000 feet early in the afternoon.

The bad weather on February 18 thwarted all but 28 FM sorties. It also delayed Task Force 58, which arrived too late to mount a single sortie. As well, 36 B-24s were recalled to their base. One fast carrier task group was able to batter Chichi Jima.

At 2130 hours on February 18, in the only incident of its kind off Iwo Jima, several IJN bombers, no doubt dispatched from Japan, attacked and damaged a troop transport, a minesweeper, and a salvage tug. Casualties aboard the three vessels mounted to 49 killed and 69 wounded.

*   *   *

There was a really big fly in the ointment of the preinvasion bombardment plan, particularly with respect to naval gun-

These three photos were taken from the "old" battleship USS *Arkansas* on February 17 and 18, 1945, in the final run-up to D-day. The *Arkansas* blanketed an area on the southwestern quadrant of the island that included Suribachi. The battleship wielded a 14-inch main battery, 5-inch secondary batteries, and an array of 20mm and 40mm antiaircraft guns that could at times be laid directly on targets ashore. The third photo, taken on February 18, shows a white phosphorous marking round as it impacts on the mountain. The main battery, which has just fired to the left (north) of Suribachi, will be adjusted by references to the marker round.
Official USN Photos

A dual-25mm antiaircraft gun emplacement overlooking Beach Yellow lies in ruins after taking a direct hit. Sporting little or no overhead cover, antiaircraft emplacements were easy targets that tended to take the brunt of fire. Larger positions with bigger guns could be seen only rarely, so the preinvasion bombardment tended toward area saturation in search of lucky hits. Note the stone-lined entry to a crew shelter and ammunition bunker in the right center area of this photo.
Official USMC Photo

fire. The Marine commander of the invasion was Lieutenant General Holland M. Smith, commanding general of Fleet Marine Force, Pacific. Smith was not only the senior Marine in the Pacific Theater, he also was the Marine Corps' most experienced amphibious assault commander. Having started his run with too little advance bombardment at Tarawa in November 1943, Smith had become an avid—and vivid—proponent for more than enough. After weighing his wishes against the requirements of operational security so close to Japan, Smith's gunfire request had been for a temperate—adequate but perhaps not overwhelming—ten days of deliberate naval gunfire with the goal of getting at Iwo's many hard-to-reach nooks and crannies with a reasonable chance of crippling the defenses.

Smith's boss, the brilliant Vice Admiral Richmond Kelly Turner, was the navy's master invasion planner, albeit a prickly authentic son of a bitch who took counsel from no one but himself. Turner had overseen the Guadalcanal invasion of August 1942, from which he both had much to learn and had learned much. He had overseen the New Georgia invasion in June 1942, and he had been Holland Smith's boss at Tarawa in November 1943. Tarawa had taught Smith to use *enough* preinvasion naval gunfire, and it and subsequent operations should have resolved any lingering technical questions Turner might have had prior to 1943.

But for reasons he kept largely to himself, Turner came back to Smith on November 15, 1944, with an offer to pummel Iwo with naval gunfire commencing on February 16—three days instead of ten. And Smith's reasoned advice, that D-day could be delayed somewhat if on-the-spot analysis said it should, went by the board.

Smith was no shrinking violet. His initials, H. M., had been fashioned into a fitting sobriquet by his troops: Howlin' Mad. Smith was every bit the son of a bitch that Turner was, but he also was Turner's subordinate. Under those circumstances, Smith bit back a

This blockhouse, overlooking one of the central beaches, was ripped by a cluster of 7.2-inch rockets fired at close range. Damage is severe and many of the troops manning it were no doubt killed, injured, or knocked silly. If this installation had been covered with earth—as were nearly all other large battle structures—there is no way the same rockets would have done much, if any, real damage. *Official USMC Photo*

direct response and asked his chief subordinate, the rather more temperate commanding general of V Amphibious Corps (VAC), Major General Harry Schmidt, to develop a staff study.

Schmidt's staff produced a masterpiece of logic that, bottom line, allowed that nine very busy days might suffice for the final crescendo of bombardments, coupled with such last-minute flourishes as an on-the-spot, up-to-the-minute beach survey and placement of inshore navigation markers by Marine reconnaissance troops and U.S. Navy underwater demolitions teams (UDTs).

This view of the eastern fleet anchorage, which also covers the route of many D-day landing vehicles and boats, was taken after D-day through a blasted viewing port in the wall of a bunker that protected a 5-inch gun employed as antiboat defense. The emplacement probably was taken out by direct naval fire or air attack in the run-up to the invasion. *Official USMC Photo*

Turner rejected the VAC revised plan out of hand and made no counteroffer. Harry Schmidt next asked for a four-day bombardment, a proposal seconded with grave misgivings by Holland Smith. Turner appears to have been on the verge of agreeing, but the compromise was dashed when Admiral Raymond Spruance, the Fifth Fleet commander and thus Turner's and Smith's and Schmidt's big boss, demurred. In Spruance's mind, the purely operational carrier interdiction of Japanese air bases on Honshu had morphed into an extravaganza in which the interdiction was relegated to a place equal to but not ahead of other—strategic—imperatives. Spruance refused to allow the surface warships or escort carriers to arrive off Iwo until the fast carriers were off Japan—to prevent an overwhelming and crippling air attack *from* Japan. He also felt that the lengthy bombing campaign against Iwo would leave the defenders dizzy with combat fatigue and left moping in ruined defenses to be rolled up by the immense weight of nearly three Marine divisions. Finally, Spruance argued that the ammunition expended during a protracted naval bombardment could not be replaced in time for the planned D-day crescendo. Given the U.S. Navy's unbelievably advanced at-sea revictualing capability, it is difficult to see how this was remotely an issue.

The Marine commanders endured several more rounds of reasoned debate, but they got back only stony silence from their navy bosses. And then events overran desires; it literally became too late to assemble the ships and stores the Marines felt would barely suffice.

To top it off, two of the three days set aside for the final prelanding bombardment were largely voided by bad weather that all but grounded the escort carrier squadrons and shaved a day from Task Force 58's contribution. Small wonder in a northern sea in the dead of winter.

Not to worry: as they had before—always—Marines armored in the shirts on their backs would dutifully advance to their deaths and ultimate glory, right over the obstacles laid before them by old men safe in the rear.

American deaths during the Iwo Jima campaign spiraled up to a staggering, unprecedented, heartbreaking 6,821. The wounded mounted up to 19,217. Now we know several reasons why, and those who bear responsibility.

It wasn't all for nothing. This 5-inch gun bunker overlooking the invasion beaches was knocked out before D-day by a direct hit from a large-caliber shell. *Official USMC Photo*

CHAPTER 5

A Mighty Armada

The Iwo Jima operation, dubbed Operation DETACHMENT, was to have been the largest amphibious operation undertaken by the Marine Corps to date. It turned out to be the largest Marine operation of World War II and, indeed, ever.

Three Marine divisions, operating under V Amphibious Corps (VAC), were earmarked for DETACHMENT. Major General Clifton Cates's 4th Marine Division, veterans of the seizure of Kwajalein Atoll in early 1944 and Saipan and Tinian in mid-1944, was to land three battalions abreast in the first waves on the right-flank beaches—Yellow-1, Yellow-2, and Blue-1; attack inland; then pivot to the right with its left flank about 60 percent of the way across the island; and proceed to the O-1 objective line, about halfway along Motoyama Airfield No. 2. Major General Keller Rockey's 5th Marine Division, which was on its maiden (and only) Pacific War operation, was to land three battalions abreast on the VAC left-flank beaches—Green, Red-1, and Red-2—and attack inland all the way across Iwo's narrow southern neck. The 28th Marines, which had at its core a solid contingent of former parachutists who were veterans of the Solomons campaign, would throw its own line across the island and attack toward Mount Suribachi. The 26th and 27th Marines would turn north on the 4th Division's left and attack to the O-1 line.

That was the plan for D-day. In reserve during the initial landing operation was Major General Graves Erskine's 3d Marine Division, which still retained a large core of veterans from the late 1943 invasion of Bougainville and the mid-1944 invasion of Guam. It was presumed that all or most of the 3d Division would be committed to the fighting on Iwo, but it was not known how much or where.

It is January 2, 1945. A 5th Marine Division war dog and his handler, a navy chief hospital corpsman, go aboard a transport bound for Iwo Jima. This war dog's specialty is carrying enough blood plasma to treat eight wounded men. *Official USMC Photo*

It is January 7, 1945. A small swing band composed of members of the 26th Marines is serenading shipmates with music of the day. *Official USMC Photo*

The special nature of DETACHMENT resulted in the presence of the highest Marine Corps field headquarters in the Pacific—Lieutenant General Holland Smith's Fleet Marine Force, Pacific (FMFPac). Smith had stood up FMFPac in the field right after he oversaw the Saipan operation as VAC commanding general. Taking his place as VAC commander was Major General Harry Schmidt, who had commanded the 4th Marine Division at Kwajalein and Saipan.

The staff and command positions of FMFPac, VAC, and the three divisions were filled to brimming with tested men. Cates—who was destined to be the first postwar Commandant of the Marine Corps—was a highly decorated veteran of fighting in France in World War I and had commanded an infantry regiment at Guadalcanal. Cate's division operations officer (his chief planner) was Colonel Alfred Pollack, who had commanded a battalion under Cates at Guadalcanal. The VAC operations officer, Colonel Edward Craig, had commanded a regiment of the 3d Marine Division at Bougainville and Guam. The staffs were filled with veterans, and virtually every regiment and battalion was commanded by a veteran. Colonel Harry Liversedge, the commanding officer of the 28th Marines, had commanded a Marine Raider regiment in the Solomons; his executive officer, Lieutenant Colonel Robert Williams, had commanded a parachute battalion at Guadalcanal and the parachute regiment later in the Solomons; and the regimental operations officer, Major Oscar Peatross, was a former Marine Raider who had been on the Makin Raid in mid-1942. And on and on. This late in the war, the sharpest minds and most aggressive personalities—all filtered by three years of hard combat—had risen to positions of leadership.

In addition to three strong, well-led, and well-equipped divisions, VAC itself fielded a variety of combat-support and service-support units deemed essential to the success of so vast, complicated, and ambitious an undertaking. These included its own communications battalion, its own medical battalion, an evacuation hospital, its own engineer battalion, a field depot, two 155mm howitzer battalions overseen by an artillery headquarters, an armored amphibian tractor battalion, four amphibian tractor battalions, a reinforced

bomb disposal company, and five 1,250-man replacement drafts that would serve as shore party and general labor pools as they were drawn down to provide replacements to the divisions. VAC also fielded an array of smaller units that were attached down to the division. These included a provisional rocket detachment, war dog platoons, special intelligence teams from the Pacific Theater joint intelligence command, and joint assault signal companies (JASCO) to direct naval and air support. One U.S. Army company equipped with the new DUKW amphibian trucks also was attached to VAC, and one apiece was attached to the 4th and 5th Marine divisions, each of which fielded an organic Marine DUKW company. The army also provided VAC and the 4th and 5th divisions with specialized port detachments as well as a pool composed of two signal air warning companies. At the expeditionary level (FMFPac), the army further provided a reinforced field hospital and an antiaircraft gun group. An Army garrison force also sailed with the invasion force for

It is February 3, 1945. These Marines, who are serving with the 28th Marines, are whiling away the long sea journey playing a no-doubt endless game of cards. Look closely at their faces. They are very young men, perhaps all teenagers. *Official USMC Photo*

When all else fails to divert the mind on a long sea journey to a dangerous place, close down and sunbathe. The journey to Iwo Jima will be the last chance these young Marines will ever have to just be young. *Official USMC Photo*

Major General Clifton Cates, the 4th Marine Division commander (center, standing), poses with members of his senior staff as they pore over a model of the objective. *Official USMC Photo*

deployment in the postbattle phase, which would include ongoing mopping-up operations by a veteran independent infantry regiment. To oversee and build airfield, port, and fuel facilities, the U.S. Navy stood up a naval construction (Seabee) brigade headquarters to oversee ten Seabee battalions, including one each attached out to VAC and the 4th and 5th Marine divisions.

Each Marine division was composed of three infantry regiments of three infantry battalions apiece; an artillery regiment of four battalions equipped with 75mm pack howitzers or 105mm field howitzers; and division service-support or combat-support units that included an engineer battalion, a medical battalion, a motor transport battalion, a pioneer (shore party) battalion, a service battalion, and a tank battalion. Before sailing for Iwo, each division was issued 2,500 replacements as a down payment on casualties. At the discretion of the division commander, these troops could be held in reserve, held back for shore labor, or used to fatten some units in advance of the landings.

* * *

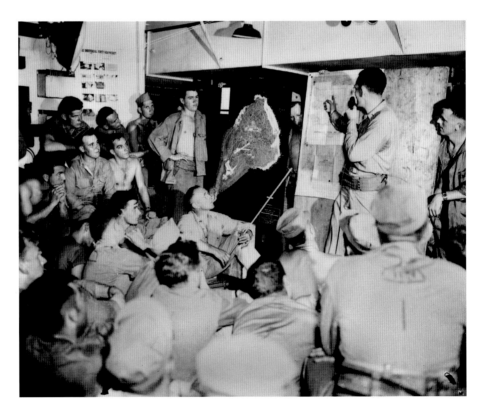

A 4th Marine Division platoon gathers for a final briefing by the platoon leader. *Official USMC Photo*

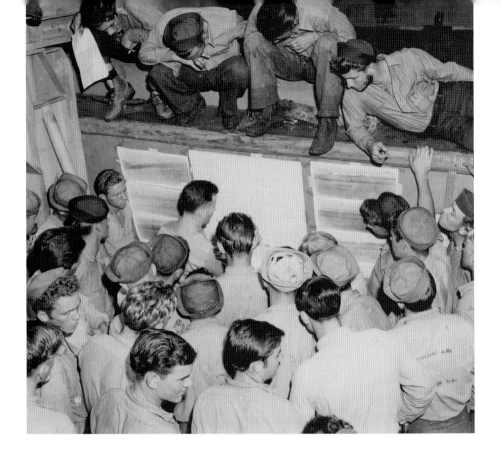

It is February 18, 1945. A navy ensign gives a final briefing to the landing craft coxswains under his command. H-hour is in the morning. *Official USMC Photo*

Following months of intense training and experimenting with new tables of organization and equipment upgrades, the invaders sailed from numerous ports throughout the Pacific and the coastal United States, all timed to bring them offshore Iwo Jima as required by a delicate schedule made more delicate by the knowledge that Iwo was well within the range of a kamikaze—or even conventional two-way—air assault from many, many airfields in Japan. On the way out, 70,647 Marines and navy hospital corpsmen assigned to FMFPac, VAC, and the three Marine divisions worked on their weapons and gear while they absorbed the latest updates in intelligence and planning, as did everyone in every ship of the mighty armada that would assemble off Iwo in its own time, from the mighty battleships and carriers to the tiny patrol craft that would control the hundreds of troop-carrying amphibian tractors (amtracs), landing craft, and landing ships to Iwo's six hot beaches. In all, Vice Admiral Richmond Kelly Turner exercised command authority over 495 ships, including the entire bombardment force, transports, LSTs, and LSMs. When supply and auxiliary ships and Task Force 58 were factored in the U.S. naval presence off Iwo would jump to nearly eight hundred ships. And, in all, nearly 250,000 Americans would be offshore Iwo Jima as the landings got under way.

Sunset at sea.
Official U.S. Coast Guard Photo

CHAPTER 6

First to Fight

The first Americans to touch ground at Iwo Jima were members of the U.S. Navy's Underwater Demolitions Team (UDT) 13. During the late afternoon of February 16, the first full day of the final bombardment cycle, these frogmen proceeded in small boats to Higashi Rock, about 2,600 yards off the eastern invasion beaches. There they placed a flashing light marker to be used as a guide by the approaching waves of amtracs and landing craft on D-day. Japanese troops on Iwo who spotted the frogmen opened fire on them, but all hands returned safely to their ship.

On February 17, at about 0800 hours, twelve wooden-hulled minesweepers approached to within 750 yards of the eastern beaches to begin a methodical search for mines as well as to check for reefs, shoals, and manmade underwater obstacles undisclosed by aerial reconnaissance. Japanese atop Mount Suribachi opened fire on the minesweepers with small arms.

At 0840 on February 17, three battleships and numerous fire-support vessels moved to within 3,000 yards of various sectors around Iwo to provide close-in support of another foray by a team of frogmen. Japanese whose big guns had remained silent to that point opened fire as the ships and gunships came within pointblank range. The battleship USS *Tennessee* was struck off southeastern Iwo by one round a little before 0900. Four sailors were injured, but damage was negligible. Within thirty minutes, as the cruiser USS *Pensacola* approached to within 1,500 yards of the northeastern shore to support the minesweepers, one Japanese 150mm gun crew opened fire on her, splashing their first round only 50 yards short of the ship. The cruiser attempted to evade, but the gunners knew their job and managed to fire six rounds into her within three minutes. Seventeen

On the morning of February 17, 1945, a wooden-hulled minesweeper (dark ship to the left) works under fire from shore batteries while a destroyer rushes in to blanket the beach at the far right with counterfire. *Official USN Photo*

officers and men were killed (including her executive officer) and 120 were wounded, her combat information center was knocked out, an observation plane on her starboard catapult was set aflame, and she was hulled in several places. For all that, as repair parties fanned out throughout the ship, the *Pensacola's* guns ceased firing only as required during the course of delicate surgeries on a number of her wounded.

Although the plucky minesweepers were dogged throughout their mission by gunfire from the island, they drew off only when their mission was completed. They found no mines and no under water obstructions.

At nearly 1100 hours, a hundred swimmers from four UDTs entered the water to make a final check of the invasion beaches for underwater obstacles and to get a close-up sense of tide and surf. They were to destroy any obstacles, natural or manmade, that they could find. The frogmen were covered by fire from twelve LCI(G) gunboats firing 20mm and 40mm guns and LCI(R) rocket ships firing clusters of 7.2-inch bombardment rockets as well as 20mm and 40mm guns. The LCIs

LCI(G) gunboats armed with 20mm and 40mm rapid-fire cannon parade toward Iwo to fire at shore targets. This photo was taken on D-day, but undoubtedly at least a few of the gunboats shown here took part in the toe-to-toe gun duel on February 17. *Official USN Photo*

closed to within 1,000 yards of the shore as the swimmers approached the beach and opened fire.

Many Japanese who watched the LCIs open fire thought the invasion was about to begin—how could they think otherwise, after all the other action that morning?—and, in direct contravention to their commanding general's orders and oft-stated wishes, they took to defending the beaches. Heavy guns overlooking and backing the landing beaches reached out to the LCIs over a period of 45 minutes. All twelve vessels were hit, some brutally, but even after drawing off to quench fires and succor the wounded, several LCIs nosed back into the toe-to-toe brawl, their crews unwilling to concede anything to the Japanese. In the meantime, destroyers and other fire-support vessels blotted out any gun emplacement they could locate or fired white phosphorous rounds to create a smoke screen. One destroyer lost 7 killed and 33 wounded to a direct hit, and the cumulative loss to the LCIs was 7 killed and 153 wounded. While all the LCIs survived the melee, only six eventually returned to Saipan under their own power.

While the navy frogmen did their work inshore and the LCIs withdrew, the battleship USS *Nevada* got into a counterbattery duel with the heavier emplacements engaging the LCIs. This went on until 1240. Three other battleships supported the frogmen by laying smoke all across the eastern beaches. The smoke was good for the frogmen, but it masked targets ashore for the many warships that had pushed their way into the fray.

All but one frogman had returned safely to their destroyer-transports by 1220 to report that the beaches were clear of mines and obstacles, and beach and surf conditions were reported as favorable. Several daredevils returned with soil samples they had had to crawl out of the water to collect.

A dead 40mm gunner aboard an LCI(G) is still draped over his gun and a wounded sailor is confined to a stretcher as other crewmen make fast to a larger ship that has come alongside to provide aid.
Official USN Photo

Lieutenant Junior Grade Rufus G. Herring of LCI(G) 449. *Official USN Photo*

The frogmen, now joined by 22 Marines from the FMFPac Reconnaissance Battalion, kicked off at 1615 to survey alternate landing beaches along Iwo's western shore. Fire protection was undertaken by three battleships and a cruiser, but the Japanese opened fire with only rifles and machine guns. No doubt, General Kuribayashi had restored fire discipline to his ranks, because wherever a heavy emplacement had been located during the morning free-for-all the Americans had plotted it and delivered heavy fire on it.

All frogmen and Marines had returned safely by 1800. They had gathered all the required data and had located and destroyed just one mine.

The Japanese who witnessed the day's action were certain they had driven off an honest-to-goodness invasion attempt. That's what Radio Tokyo announced that very night, along with news that Japanese gunners had sunk a battleship and five lesser warships.

The Japanese announcement was good for a laugh around the invasion fleet, but no one was laughing in flag country aboard the American warships. The day's action had proven beyond a doubt that Iwo was honeycombed with hidden large fortifications that would require days of careful attention and more windfall action to locate, much less neutralize. The admiral commanding the bombardment force authorized the gun-fire ships to dip into their ammunition reserves for the February 18 bombardment, but that was the last chance anyone had to *really* soften Iwo before the Marines stormed the beaches.

The Marine commanders, Holland Smith and Harry Schmidt, had been right from the get-go: ten days of heavy bombardment *might* have sufficed and a possible rolling delay for the landings *might* have done the trick and saved many lives and limbs. But the navy com-manders, Raymond Spruance and Kelly Turner, had painted the Marines into a terrible cor-ner and had thus issued death warrants for nearly seven thousand of their countrymen.

Gunners aboard a U.S. Navy LCI(R) rocket gunboat take a break. Note that the gunners at left have protected their faces and hands with antiflash ointment. *Official USN Photo*

CHAPTER 7

Ship to Shore

D-day at Iwo Jima—February 19, 1945—started with what was to be the biggest one-day shore bombardment of the Pacific War. The fast carriers had arrived on station the evening before and had dispatched many of their larger escorts to Iwo to add their voices to those of the bombardment vessels that had arrived on February 16. The first Fifth Fleet vessels—ranging up to two fast battleships armed with nine 16-inch guns apiece and six older battleships armed with 14-inch guns—opened fire at 0640. By then, Task Force 53, the invasion armada conveying the Marines to Iwo, also had arrived to begin putting the troops into the water. At 0730, 42 LCI(R)s with 4.5-inch and 5-inch rockets and LCI(G)s with 4.2-inch mortars, 40mm, and 20mm guns surged inshore to open fire. The little LCI bombardment craft alone would expend ten thousand rockets and heavy mortar rounds in only a few hours.

By 0725, LSTs had put all 482 troop-carrying amtracs carrying 8 reinforced Marine infantry battalions into the water. At 0800, the warships checked fire to make way for a strike by 120 fighters and light bombers from Task Force 58. Among these were 24 VMF-124 F4U Corsair fighter-bombers from the USS *Essex*, each armed with rockets, napalm, and six .50-caliber machine guns. The warships used the recess to reposition themselves even closer inshore, then resumed firing as the carrier planes pulled away at 0825. In less than 30 minutes, the warships, large and small, sent off 8,000 shells and rockets into the invasion beaches alone, then shifted inland to create what was planned to become a rolling barrage 400 yards ahead of the advancing ground troops.

For their part, the 482 troop-carrying amtracs and 68 LVT(A)-4 armored amtracs began moving toward the line of departure two miles offshore a little after 0800 and signaled

A submarine's-eye view of Iwo Jima shows the eastern invasion beaches pretty much as they would look to the onrushing first wave of Marines bound for the island. Mount Suribachi is to the left. Photographs like this as well as aerial photos were used to construct maps and models used by Marine planners, for training, and by U.S. Navy gunfire planners. This photo was part of a series taken by the submarine USS *Spearfish* between November 29 and December 2, 1944. Markings on the periscope sight reticule can be seen at top, bottom, and sides. *Official USN Photo*

This aerial portrait of Iwo Jima, taken months after the battle, provides an excellent perspective on the D-day objectives. The right side of the island is the eastern side, and the landing beaches run all along the more or less straight stretch in the middle foreground. From the bottom (southeast) to top (northeast) beaches, the vanguard battalions are to be the 5th Marine Division's 1st Battalion, 28th Marines (1/28); 2d Battalion, 27th Marines (2/27); and 1st Battalion, 27th Marines (1/27); then the 4th Marine Division's 1st Battalion, 23d Marines (1/23); 2d Battalion, 23d Marines (2/23); 1st Battalion, 25th Marines (1/25); and 3d Battalion, 25th Marines (3/25). *National Archives & Records Administration*

at 0815 that they were ready to cross the line. At 0830, on the mark, the leading control vessel dipped her pennant to signal the first wave of amtracs onward. It was about 4,000 yards to the beaches, a 30-minute ride. The second amtrac wave crossed the line 250 to 300 yards behind the first, and the third wave took the same interval behind the second, on up to eight waves mounted in amtracs and then LCVPs and larger landing craft. The plan was to get 9,000 troops ashore within a 45-minute period, give them a little time to re-form and open the advance to the D-day objectives, then follow on with tanks, artillery, more troops, and all the accouterments of war felt to be vital by that phase of the Pacific War. The generals hoped the show would be over "in a few days."

D-day morning. An LVT(A)-4 armored amphibian tractor mounting a short-barrel 75mm gun is about to be swayed out over the side of its transport and lowered into the water to begin its journey ashore. The armored amtracs were designed to keep pace with the initial waves of troop-carrying amtracs, to provide tank-like covering power either from just offshore or alongside infantry on the beach. A total of 68 LVT(A)-4s from the 2d Armored Amphibian Battalion are to accompany the first waves of troop-carrying amtracs to all the invasion beaches. *Official USMC Photo*

Marines of 1/26, part of the 5th Marine Division reserve, begin to climb down the sides of their transport to a waiting LCVP via cargo nets. *Official USMC Photo*

As the leading amtrac wave closed to about 400 yards from the beaches, the Marine Corsairs returned for a final strafing run at exceptionally low level, the better to keep Japanese heads down at the critical juncture. It was a bravura performance, Marine to Marine. As amtrac cleats bit into surfside sand, the Marine pilots flicked their control sticks and resighted on targets about 500 yards inland.

The first wave landed between 0859 and 0903, and the second came ashore two minutes later. So far, the Japanese had not opened fire.

This 4th Marine Division flamethrower assaultman is still having a good time. He has named the pinup on his back "Miss Spitfire." *Official USMC Photo*

Each LCVP could convey about forty fully equipped Marines—such as a reinforced platoon—from their transport to the beach. *Official USMC Photo*

Most troop-carrying amtracs were conveyed to Iwo Jima in the same LSTs in which the lead assault troops were embarked. This convenience, which began in the Marshalls in early 1944, made it a simple matter for Marines to climb into their assigned amtracs and ride them out into the water over the LST's extended bow ramp. Note in the photo above that a wartime censor has covered the amtrac's ID number, but the same was not done in the photo below. *Official USMC Photos*

Marines also embarked on the last leg of the journey to Iwo aboard the new DUKW amphibian truck. This DUKW belongs to the 5th Marine Division's 5th Amphibian Truck Company, and the passengers are members of the division's artillery regiment, the 13th Marines. The DUKWs and artillery units were a good fit because the vehicle could carry a 105mm howitzer or a large cargo of ammunition all the way to shore from an LST, while an amtrac could carry only a disassembled 75mm pack howitzer and much less ammunition. Most artillery and ammunition, however, had to be carried to the beach aboard landing craft. *Official USMC Photo*

It is 0828 on February 19, 1945. The invasion is shaping up. As warships on the horizon, including at least one battleship, pummel the landing beaches and high ground, armored amtracs form up at the line of departure. They will soon be dispersed among the troop-carrying amtracs for the run to the beach in the very first wave to land. *Official USMC Photo*

Amtracs loaded with 4th Marine Division infantrymen and assault engineers pass a transport on their way to land at the forefront of the invasion force. *Official USMC Photo*

It appears that the little amtracs must negotiate a confusing maze of high-sided transports, cargo ships, LSTs, and other seagoing vessels, but each large ship has been precisely placed, and the "roads" through them are also precise. If everything is in the right place, no one will get lost. *Official USMC Photo*

The mood aboard this Iwo-bound LCVP is still relaxed. The troops have placed their gear on the deck, which for now is a good thing, because if their LCVP sinks they can use the life belts they all have around their waists. If someone with full battle gear on deploys a life belt in the water he is likely to turn over head-down because he will be so top-heavy. *Official USMC Photo*

These troop-filled amtracs are now in open water beyond the larger transport and cargo vessels. All the troops can see out ahead is bombardment vessels, control vessels, and Iwo Jima. *Official USMC Photo*

LCVPs and some larger landing craft conduct a delicate ballet to get properly formed up for the run to the beach. Grouped according to their places in the assault formation, LCVPs—typically from the same ship—circle in a holding pattern while other boats are loaded and then join up. The outer circle of boats at the top right are uncoiling from the holding pattern to begin the run on the beach. *Official USN Photo*

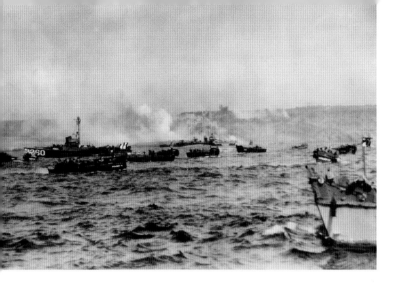

This view toward the fire-swept invasion beaches shows LCVPs circling near one of the small control vessels (left center) charged with orchestrating and sequencing the traffic for each beach. *Official USMC Photo*

As they approach the bombardment battle line, the Marines aboard this LCVP have their helmets and packs on, and they look more pensive than before. No wonder: Iwo is dead ahead. *Official USMC Photo*

It is time to go. Further control is provided by this navy or coast guard signalman. This LCVP probably is commanded by a landing craft division officer charged with overseeing a small flotilla of landing craft from one ship. There are hundreds of identical-looking LCVPs in the water, and no end of potential screw-ups in the offing. Control *has* to be tight. Note that in addition to its own ID number, this LCVP is showing a placard at the bow and a large flag aft to further identify itself to its own group of landing craft. *Official USMC Photo*

This little group of amtracs is carrying a first-wave assault platoon toward the bombardment battle line.
Official USMC Photo

Fourth Marine Division first-wave amtracs, aligned nearly to the horizon, are passing the last line of control vessels. Only the bombardment battle line lies between them and Iwo.
Official USMC Photo

Progress check: The leading edge of the first wave of amtracs and armored amtracs is approaching the bombardment battle line. A battleship at right center and smaller warships spread in both directions are firing directly at the beach in what amounts to final preparatory fires. They will shortly shift to area saturation farther inland. The amtracs can now be reached by Japanese guns ashore, but the Japanese gunners have no doubt been disciplined for their unruly behavior on February 17, and not one shot is fired at the warships or the oncoming assault amtracs. *Official USN Photo*

Now the first wave of troop-carrying amtracs is passing one of the battleships as she fires a broadside from her port 5-inch secondary battery and, perhaps, her aft 14-inch turret. *Official USMC Photo*

Amtracs are out ahead as this clutch of LCVPs, probably with a reinforced infantry company spread across it, opens out and aligns itself into assault formation for the final dash to the beach. The LCVPs are about to pass a destroyer that is still firing directly at the beach. *Official USMC Photo*

The first wave of amtracs is now fully committed, pounding toward the beach with everything they have. All the troops and crewmen have their heads down except the .50-caliber machine gunners. These amtracs are well within the zone of maximum vulnerability from machine guns, small arms, and antiboat guns in the hands of beachside defenders in hidden pillboxes and bunkers. As yet, however, the defenders have not fired a shot. *Official USMC Photo*

At almost the last moment before touchdown, a quadruple-40mm mount aboard one of the battleships fires directly into Beach Green, right over the heads of the men of 1/28. *Official USN Photo*

It is 0859 hours. At the far left of the line, the amtracs carrying 1/28 to Beach Green have surged ahead of the units to their right and are just seconds away from touchdown. *Official USN Photo*

CHAPTER 8

Beach Assault

Nothing happened. There was no return fire. No Japanese fired at the ships offshore, nor at the oncoming waves of amtracs, nor at the assaulting Marines who were surprised to learn as their feet touched down that all of southern Iwo Jima was covered in a thick mantle of black volcanic ash—not simply black sand. The ash offered no purchase for their feet or their shovels.

Ahead lay another surprise: a 15-foot terrace that rose sharply from just in back of the beaches. Most of the armored amtracs, which fired their 75mm guns as they landed, did not have enough speed on to scale this slippery slope; some did, but many others returned to the water and fired on the few suspect features the gunners could see.

Wave upon wave landed on eerily safe beaches. Three Marine divisions had come to fight for Iwo Jima, and two-thirds of two of them appeared to be getting a free pass.

*   *   *

Between 0900 and 1000 hours, the Japanese response to the landing was disciplined; the only really big opposition was heavy mortar fire set against 2/23 on Beach Yellow-2, which began within three minutes of the first wave hitting the beach. At about 0935, Beaches Green, Red-1, and Red-2, in the 5th Marine Division zone, were struck by opening mortar salvoes. And at about 0940, some 150 yards inland from Beach Green, 1/28 began to take a rising crescendo of mortar concentrations, but these troops were by then getting into a built-up area of blockhouses, bunkers, pillboxes, and other fixed positions; of course the Japanese defenders gave it their all.

An LVT(A)-4 armored amtrac accompanies the first troops of 2/27 to land on Beach Red-2 at about 0900 hours, February 19, 1945. There is no response at all from the defenders. *Official USMC Photo*

A reinforced Marine infantry company has just landed on one of the center beaches. According to the plan, these troops will hunker down and reorganize until more troops from their battalion have landed behind them. Note that amtracs at the water's edge have just landed another company. *Official USMC Photo*

More follow-on troops have landed, so the lead companies bound forward to the next line of cover. By now, Marines have discovered that the so-called black sand is really volcanic ash in which it is difficult for heavily burdened assault troops to gain secure footing. So far, the Japanese have not opened fire. *Official USMC Photo*

These 4th Division gunners are advancing to the front to join the leading assault rifleman. In the right foreground is a Marine's gear; the owner might have been shot by a Japanese infantryman in a nearby position. So far, only individual and small groups of Japanese on the spot have opened fire. Otherwise, this is a textbook landing that is evolving pretty much as planned. *Official USMC Photo*

The descent to hell began as the lead infantry units on the left and in the center advanced up the terrace and forward to points about 500 yards inland. Then the world fell in on them as prearranged fires overseen by steady leaders and directed by stoic forward observers erupted on and around every living Marine and American mechanical aid on the landing beaches. Japanese machine gunners and riflemen, hitherto hunkered down in caves or fighting positions, opened fire on Marines advancing across open ground.

The Marines fell to the ground, looking for targets or looking after their wounds. Those who tried to dig in found that the volcanic ash could not be moved without moving back. Immediately, a great hue and cry went up: send us sandbags. There was no way to dig in and no means at hand to build shelter. Marines had walked into the kill zone, and they were being killed.

There was mayhem at the beach. Infantry could manage after a fashion; there was always a way to get forward on foot, but anything with wheels sank to its axles in the volcanic ash. Even the treads on tanks and amtracs slipped and dug into the bottomless ash.

These 5th Division Marines are warily approaching the summit of the 15-foot terrace that backs most of the landing beaches. The terrace is excellent cover for now, but the slippery volcanic ash makes it very difficult to negotiate while carrying full combat gear. *Official USMC Photo*

It is not quite time to resume the advance as follow-on waves arrive with mortars, tanks, and other support weapons. As some Marines keep an eye on the hostile terrain ahead, others begin to experiment with digging into the liquidlike volcanic ash. *Official USMC Photo*

Air and artillery continue to pound Mount Suribachi as, in its shadow on Beach Green—and no doubt under observation from the heights—the two leading battalions of the 28th Marines prepare to jump off to Iwo Jima's far shore. *Official USMC Photo*

At the other end of the beachhead, 1/25 and 3/25 have landed abreast on Beach Blue-1 to find the beach less treacherous all around than the beaches to their left. (Note how relaxed the smoker looks.) The two veteran battalions, now into their fourth amphibious assault, are charged with attacking northward along the beach to seize Blue-2 on foot and then advance through a shell-cratered moonscape toward the Rock Quarry to anchor the entire VAC line. So far there has been little gunfire heard on the Marine far right flank. *Official USMC Photos*

In at least one case, the front wheels of a vehicle dug in as soon as they left the ramp of a landing craft, and that pinned the ramp to the beach, preventing the craft from retracting under the intense mortar and artillery fire. As the day progressed, a high inshore tide just made things worse, and scores of landing craft broached in the surf and foundered.

* * *

At the front, the infantry quickly adapted to the harsh realities of Iwo Jima. Infantrymen always adapt; they are the best adapters in the world, for if they cannot or will not or even do not adapt, they die. They couldn't dig in, and they certainly could not withdraw to the shell-struck mayhem on the beaches. So they attacked. They attacked every fighting position they could both see and reach, and then they went looking for more. In due course, they won ground, killed defenders, and advanced toward their D-day objectives. The reserve battalions were landed and thrown into the fight at the front or sent to clear bypassed positions behind the front. In due course, tanks, armored amtracs, 75mm halftracks, and 37mm guns, even 75mm howitzers, found their way to the front. But it was the brave infantry who took the ground from other brave infantry, all of them heedless of their lives.

Back at the landing beaches, and now under small-arms fire, larger landing craft and landing ships (an LSM is shown) have begun to land combat-support troops, tanks (at far left), and jeeps and trucks preloaded with water and ammunition. Unfortunately, as amtrac crews discovered early on, it is difficult for even tracked vehicles to find purchase in the volcanic ash. The beginnings of beach congestion are evident in this view of a 4th Marine Division beach taken a little after 1000 hours, but so far the congestion is not as crippling as it had been in virtually all earlier amphibious operations.
Official USMC Photo

And then the sky fell in: the Japanese, no doubt on orders from General Kuribayashi, opened fire with every mortar, gun, and rocket launcher that could reach the landing beaches as well as Marine combat units, which had advanced out to about 500 yards at the point of deepest penetration. *Official USMC Photo*

Within little more than an hour after the first waves landed, rear-echelon troops have begun to get the beach organized to receive huge cargoes of supplies, combat- and service-support troops, and various headquarters units. In this case, engineers wearing antiflash ointment on their faces have begun to clear mines from tape-defined paths to inland dump sites and preplanned artillery emplacements. These 5th Division engineers use knives and fingers to search for ceramic-cased mines that cannot be found by metal-seeking mine detectors. *Official USMC Photo*

At Iwo Jima's narrowest point, two companies of 1/28 drove to the western shore with a costly gallantry that cannot be described in terms that have been invented yet. Both company commanders led small teams of volunteers at the heads of their units, knocked out position after position until one of the captains collapsed from the effects of his mortal wounds and the other was incapacitated by merely "serious" wounds. In the wake of leaders such as these, Marines who lost track of their own units joined other stragglers to take out fighting positions whose interlocking bands of fire swept over all Marines, lost and found, all along and behind the front. Marine mortars with no cover and just the rounds that could be carried to them were fired directly at targets their crews could see with their own eyes—a situation that was rare on any other modern battlefield.

Six of eight Marine 75mm and 105mm howitzer battalions came ashore in dribs and drabs through the long afternoon. Guns were lost when the DUKWs conveying them to the beach took direct hits from the pervasive bombardment, or they were hit after they were

The main Japanese fires are still falling inland, but ranging shots have been falling along the beach for some time. Between rounds, dead Marines can be seen interspersed among the living (left foreground), and bursting shells can be seen beside the near LSM and farther down the beach. *Official USMC Photo*

This Marine has scrambled across a dead body and a folded litter in his quest for a safe place to hunker down. It appears that an LCVP or an amtrac has taken a direct hit right off this beach. *Official USMC Photo*

Shortly after 1000 hours, this LSM takes two direct mortar hits as it retracts from the beach after dropping off tanks of the 5th Tank Battalion. *Official USMC Photo*

A dazed Marine amtrac crewman whose vehicle has been hit offshore is handled with care by the crew of a coast guard LCVP rigged for rescue and repair work. *Official U.S. Coast Guard Photo*

Despite fires that are rising in crescendo by the moment, a follow-on infantry battalion bravely undertakes its rush inland from the surf. The handcarts these infantrymen are struggling with in the soft sand and ash carry medium machine guns and machine gun ammunition. *Official USMC Photos*

As if gunfire weren't enough to contend with, the surf conditions deteriorated dramatically as D-day wore on. Here, an LCVP has been pushed sideways by a following wave and is in danger of foundering. *Official USMC Photo*

Even though this section of beach is under fire and their LCVP has been run aground by deteriorating surf conditions, these mission-minded Marines have manhandled their machine gun cart into the surf and will carry it, if necessary, to rejoin their unit. *Official USMC Photo*

set in, or they couldn't be carried over the terrace to be set in in the first place. But slowly, using coordinates radioed in by aerial observers or forward observers at the front, or anyone at the front who could provide reliable real-time information, the guns in the beachhead took out positions that were holding up the ground advance. The Marine artillery and the mobile naval gunfire also took out Japanese guns, mortars, and observation posts, which slowly unraveled the Japanese coverage of the battlefield—created dead ground by creating dead Japanese gunners and dead Japanese mortar and artillery observers.

By 1100, ten Marines from two platoons of Company B, 1/28, joined forces on their battalion's objective, the western beach at Iwo Jima's narrowest point, some 700 yards across the narrow neck from Beach Green. Behind these brave but exhausted Marines, the men of 2/28 mopped up its zone and established a continuous line across the narrow neck, then faced the southwestern tail of the island, which was dominated by the forbidding heights of Mount Suribachi. To the right, the 27th Marines came abreast, in places only a few yards from the western shore.

On the V Amphibious Corps far right, with 4th Tank Battalion M4 Sherman tanks in the vanguard and elements of 3/24 in reserve, 3/25 advanced 300 yards along the beach

Two amtracs have been blown up here and a tank has churned itself into the sand, but the show goes on as rear-echelon troops charged with numerous beachside duties try to get set up to support the drive inland. *Official USMC Photo*

By early D-day afternoon, significant sections of the busy beaches were fouled by wrecked landing craft and amtracs as well as rolling stock and other assorted equipment and supplies. Note that a bulldozer at top left is already ashore to develop the road net that will be crucial to keeping Marines at the front in the fight. *Official USMC Photo*

The original caption to this photo reads, "As far as the eye can see Navy and Coast Guard landing craft, as well as Marine amtracs, pile into Iwo Jima's assault beach for the invasion that brings American forces another step closer to the Jap mainland. On the ridge several advance guards may be seen, while crouched just in front of the boats a group of Marines takes shelter from withering Jap machine gun fire." *Official U.S. Coast Guard Photo*

Scorched earth. These Marines have dug in on a scorched, smoldering rise in the shadow of a blown bunker (top center). Litter in the foreground and a dead Marine (bottom edge) attest to the shelling sustained along this piece of the beachhead. *Official USMC Photo*

These four photos are a sequence shot by a 5th Marine Division combat cameraman of an amtrac taking a direct hit by a mortar round. In the first photo (top right), flamethrower tanks in the center that also are hit send a huge fireball to the right. Note that an abandoned 13th Marines 75mm pack howitzer appears in the first and fourth photos. The amtrac suffers through several detonations as it is hit, as its fuel supply is ignited, and then as the fire finally detonates what is probably a cargo of ammunition.
Official USMC Photos

A brave flamethrower assaultman steps from cover and spits deadly fire at the embrasure of a large buried pillbox as fellow Marines hunker down at the foot of the structure. *Official USMC Photo*

across fairly open terrain under intense fire to reach its D-day goal near the Rock Quarry and East Boat Basin. Inland 1/25 and 2/25 swung wide from Beach Blue-1 to extend the regimental line inland, but they were driven back by intense fire and held to gains of 100 yards. By 1900, 3/25 had achieved its D-day goals at the cost of nearly eight hundred casualties and had incorporated a company each of 1/24 and 3/24 to bolster its strength. During the evening, 3/25 was relieved in place by 1/24.

By nightfall, the 4th Marine Division was bogged down in line with the northeast–southwest taxiway of Airfield No. 1, which was to have been taken in its entirety by the 23d Marines. Instead of ending D-day on a line running generally east to west across the midpoint of Iwo Jima, the two Marine divisions held a northeast-to-southwest line about halfway across the southern third of the island—less than half the ground they had planned to take.

*   *   *

(continued on page 85)

THE PRESIDENT OF THE UNITED STATES TAKES PRIDE IN PRESENTING
THE MEDAL OF HONOR TO

CORPORAL TONY STEIN
UNITED STATES MARINE CORPS RESERVE

FOR SERVICE AS SET FORTH IN THE FOLLOWING CITATION:

For conspicuous gallantry and intrepidity at the risk of his life above and beyond the call of duty while serving with Company A, 1st Battalion, 28th Marines, 5th Marine Division, in action against enemy Japanese forces on Iwo Jima, in the Volcano Islands, 19 February 1945. The first man of his unit to be on station after hitting the beach in the initial assault, Corporal Stein, armed with a personally improvised aircraft-type weapon, provided rapid covering fire as the remainder of his platoon attempted to move into position and, when his comrades were stalled by a concentrated machine-gun and mortar barrage, gallantly stood upright and exposed himself to the enemy's view, thereby drawing the hostile fire to his own person and enabling him to observe the location of the furiously blazing hostile guns. Determined to neutralize the strategically placed weapons, he boldly charged the enemy pillboxes one by one and succeeded in killing twenty of the enemy during the furious single-handed assault. Cool and courageous under the merciless hail of exploding shells and bullets which fell on all sides, he continued to deliver the fire of his skillfully improvised weapon at a tremendous rate of speed which rapidly exhausted his ammunition. Undaunted, he removed his helmet and shoes to expedite his movements and ran back to the beach for additional ammunition, making a total of eight trips under intense fire and carrying or assisting a wounded man back each time. Despite the unrelenting savagery and confusion of battle, he rendered prompt assistance to his platoon whenever the unit was in position, directing the fire of a halftrack against a stubborn pillbox until he had effected the ultimate destruction of the Japanese fortification. Later in the day, although his weapon was twice shot from his hands, he personally covered the withdrawal of his platoon to the company position. Stouthearted and indomitable, Corporal Stein, by his aggressive initiative, sound judgment and unwavering devotion to duty in the face of terrific odds, contributed materially to the fulfillment of his mission, and his outstanding valor throughout the bitter hours of conflict sustained and enhanced the highest traditions of the United States Naval Service.

Corporal Tony Stein of the 1st Battalion, 28th Marines. Stein was shot dead by a sniper on March 1. *Official USMC Photo*

Each Marine infantry company included a mortar section to be employed at the company commander's discretion. Each section fielded three 60mm mortars, each manned by a gunner, assistant gunner, and three ammunition carriers. This 4th Marine Division 60mm crew is about to fire a white phosphorous round. *Official USMC Photo*

Marine infantry reinforcements with a flamethrower assaultman attached infiltrate forward from one of the 4th Division beaches to bolster the inland assault toward Motoyama Airfield No. 1. *Official USMC Photo*

An entire flamethrower assault section rushes inland, using all available cover, to join the fight at the front. *Official USMC Photo*

Communications wiremen sprint ahead to push a telephone line through to front-line troops. Without brave men to put in the lines and keep them open, the front-line infantry would have no way to place timely calls for artillery fire or air support. *Official USMC Photo*

THE PRESIDENT OF THE UNITED STATES TAKES PRIDE IN PRESENTING THE MEDAL OF HONOR POSTHUMOUSLY TO

SERGEANT DARRELL S. COLE
UNITED STATES MARINE CORPS RESERVE

FOR SERVICE AS SET FORTH IN THE FOLLOWING CITATION:

For conspicuous gallantry and intrepidity at the risk of his life above and beyond the call of duty while serving as Leader of a Machine-gun Section of Company B, 1st Battalion, 23d Marines, 4th Marine Division, in action against enemy Japanese forces during the assault on Iwo Jima in the Volcano Islands, 19 February 1945. Assailed by a tremendous volume of small-arms, mortar and artillery fire as he advanced with one squad of his section in the initial assault wave, Sergeant Cole boldly led his men up the sloping beach toward Airfield No. 1 despite the blanketing curtain of flying shrapnel and, personally destroying with hand grenades two hostile emplacements which menaced the progress of his unit, continued to move forward until a merciless barrage of fire emanating from three Japanese pillboxes halted the advance. Instantly placing his one remaining machine gun in action, he delivered a shattering fusillade and succeeded in silencing the nearest and most threatening emplacement before his weapon jammed and the enemy, reopening fire with knee mortars and grenades, pinned down his unit for the second time. Shrewdly gauging the tactical situation and evolving a daring plan of counterattack, Sergeant Cole, armed solely with a pistol and one grenade, coolly advanced alone to the hostile pillboxes. Hurling his one grenade at the enemy in sudden, swift attack, he quickly withdrew, returned to his own lines for additional grenades and again advanced, attacked, and withdrew. With enemy guns still active, he ran the gantlet of slashing fire a third time to complete the total destruction of the Japanese strong point and the annihilation of the defending garrison in this final assault. Although instantly killed by an enemy grenade as he returned to his squad, Sergeant Cole had eliminated a formidable Japanese position, thereby enabling his company to storm the remaining fortifications, continue the advance and seize the objective. By his dauntless initiative, unfaltering courage and indomitable determination during a critical period of action, Sergeant Cole served as an inspiration to his comrades, and his stouthearted leadership in the face of almost certain death sustained and enhanced the highest traditions of the United States Naval Service. He gallantly gave his life for his country.

Sergeant Darrell S. Cole of the 1st Battalion, 23d Marines.
Official USMC Photo

Two 3/25 Marines cast their wary eyes ahead and discuss the odds as at least four 4th Tank Battalion Shermans probe forward toward 3/25's D-day objective.
Official USMC Photo

There was no end of manual labor available on the beach to help set up the artillery battalions seeking to get into action on D-day. Outgoing artillery boosted morale on a day filled with too much incoming, but it takes a lot of materials and many willing hands to dig this 105mm battery in against the slippery tide of volcanic ash that covers the beachhead area. *Official USMC Photo*

Marine infantrymen take cover in a shallow gully as an M4 medium tank probes forward on solid ground inland from the beaches. *Official USMC Photo*

At H+3 hours a Marine infantryman has staked out the entryway to a Japanese bunker with his Thompson submachine gun. It takes luck, a good eye, and a steady heart to move forward on Iwo once the shooting has started. *Official USMC Photo*

A 5th Division Marine who has been badly shocked by a nearby mortar detonation is rushed to the rear for medical attention by two buddies willing to brave fire to be sure he has not suffered grave internal injuries caused by the overpressure of the explosion that has left him without external wounds. *Official USMC Photo*

In the midst of an intense mortar barrage, a navy hospital corpsman attached to a Marine infantry platoon succors a Marine riflemen who has just been seriously wounded. *Official USMC Photo*

(continued from page 80)

The Cost

Estimates place U.S. D-day casualties at nearly 550 killed and more than 1,800 wounded or otherwise incapacitated.

This Marine examines the shell splinter that did him in. His wounds have been tended and he now awaits a stretcher to take him back to the beach for evacuation to one of the medically equipped ships and LSTs. *Official USMC Photo*

Corpsmen treat a 1/28 company first sergeant who was wounded in the back by a mortar round near Beach Green. *Official USMC Photo*

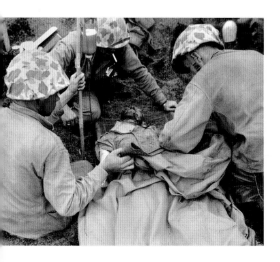

A critically wounded Marine is given plasma and intensive treatment by three corpsman who are trying to keep him alive in an impromptu beachside aid station. *Official USMC Photo*

Seven corpsman—perhaps one is a surgeon—work feverishly to keep a severely wounded Marine alive. This is probably a battalion aid station set up in a deep shellhole. The general mess attests to what has been a busy, busy day. *Official USMC Photo*

Once treated in a beachside aid station, nearly every patient must be transferred out to one of the shipboard hospitals set up in anticipation of heavy—but not *this* heavy—casualties. Litter bearers drawn from medical units or work parties must carry the wounded to the beach to load them aboard landing craft or amtracs. Then the conveyance from the beach needs to locate one of the hospital ships, where the wounded are typically swayed aboard and taken below for reassessment and follow-on treatment. It is no less busy aboard the hospital ships than it is ashore, but it is ever so much easier to work without shells dropping in. *Official USMC Photos*

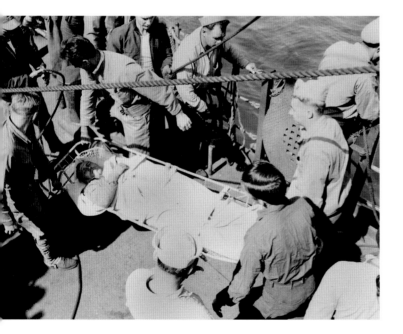

More than 1,800 Marines and sailors were rescued, treated, and saved on D-day, but an estimated 550 were killed outright or died of their wounds at Iwo Jima on February 19, 1945, alone. *Official USMC Photo*

Official USMC Photos

The Marine in this temporary grave sustained three wounds while helping his buddies take out a pillbox. It is unsafe to repatriate him to the beach, so the survivors have buried him where he fell and fixed up a marker so he can be found by graves registration troops if they are called upon to leave him. *Official USMC Photo*

Official USMC Photo

That rarest of all D-day sights, a dead Japanese soldier in the open. This infantryman was killed in his one-man position overlooking Beach Yellow and dragged into the open as a security measure as well as for passersby to see. *Official USMC Photo*

CHAPTER 9

The Marines Have Landed

The statistics for D-day were impressive: By nightfall, V Amphibious Corps had committed 30,000 men in six infantry regiments, six artillery battalions, and all or parts of approximately a dozen support battalions to Iwo Jima. Air support for the day amounted to more than 600 aircraft undertaking 26 major missions in which more than 137 tons of fragmentation bombs and more than 100 napalm bombs were administered. Nothing even close to this had ever been accomplished in the Pacific.

The assault had fallen well short of the D-day objectives, which had been based on rosy predictions that had remained unchanged even after the Fifth Fleet's decision to undertake a prelanding bombardment of only three days. Nevertheless, and despite very high casualties in return for the D-day gains, VAC was ashore in force, and the prognosis was excellent. Vital reinforcements and supplies, especially munitions, poured ashore under cover of darkness as the 4th and 5th Marine divisions rejiggered and sealed their lines against a Japanese night assault as well as to create a secure jumping-off point for continuing attacks, on February 20.

Expectations of a night assault—a "banzai"—ran extremely high. It was virtually a tradition. But General Kuribayashi had forbidden such a waste of his well-trained troops, and his edict was enforced with an iron hand. Rather, Kuribayashi had seen that special assault units were set aside and trained to undertake swift, covert raids against the American rear, against the flow of supplies and reinforcements, against the Americans' sense of accomplishment and well-being. In addition, Kuribayashi ordered that the artillery spigot be opened all the way that night—when there was little chance that his guns would be discovered and directly challenged by the support fleet's huge and numerous guns.

The 25th Marines fuel and ammunition dump was touched off by an artillery round at 0400 hours on February 20, 1945. The sky was lighted for miles around and the detonation's blast front threw men and equipment about all across a broad circle. Many members of the beach party, as well as passersby out on a hundred lonely missions, were killed, wounded, blinded, rendered deaf, or at least touched by the immense shock wave and debris cloud.
Official USMC Photo

Japanese mortars scored direct hits on two DUKWs and a jeep as they crossed paths on the beach. *Official USMC Photo*

Shore party and other rear-echelon troops have built beachside bunkers and sandbag retaining walls as far as the eye can see, but little has been done to salvage the many amtracs that came across on D-day. In this scene, two amtracs lie buried in sand in the foreground, then an armored amtrac, another amtrac, another armored amtrac, then a tank, and so on down the beach. Note that .50-caliber machine guns have been removed from the two near buried amtracs to be used to defend the beach against air and ground attack. *Official USMC Photo*

This aerial view of a 4th Marine Division beach on the morning of February 20 provides many details of the first full day ashore. The beach is largely fouled by a dozen broached landing craft of several sizes as well as a Japanese landing ship (top right) sunk by carrier air on August 4, 1944. There are many newly built sandbagged positions, including gun emplacements, extending inland to the beach terrace. At the right top, a stream of laden amtracs extends from the surf line and on out a beaten roadway toward the fighting front. *Official USMC Photo*

This view, probably from the deck of an LSM, shows another stretch of fouled beach in the 4th Marine Division zone. Two large fires blanket the skyline with thick white smoke. *Official USMC Photo*

The Americans rushed goods and troops to the crowded, half-fouled beaches while the battle-taut troops inland kept a wary watch against "banzai" attacks. Meanwhile, specially trained Japanese raiders infiltrated into the target-rich VAC rear.

An hour before midnight, the Blue and Yellow beaches in the VAC center had to be closed to landing craft and landing ships due to the sheer intensity of the shelling. At about the same time a sharp-eyed lookout spotted the contours of a *Japanese* landing barge as it approached Beach Red behind the 28th Marines, and Marine riflemen picked off 39 Japanese raiders—shot them dead. Elsewhere, other sharp-eyed Americans killed the odd infiltrator, but not enough. Among other choice targets, the Japanese raiders touched off a massive explosion in an ammunition dump and blew up a boatload of critically needed 81mm mortar ammunition on a rush priority for the front. The latter setback was so stealthy that it was thought to be the result of a lucky artillery shell fired blindly into the surf, but a captured Japanese soldier reported otherwise.

The artillery blanket, an area saturation fired by the numbers and at no particular target, was so intense that it simply had to connect with something important. One large round struck dead on the 1/23 command post on Beach Yellow, where it killed the battalion commander, the regimental operations officer, and others. The 25th Marines ammunition and fuel dump took a direct hit at about 0400 that blew it to atoms.

A steady trickle of dead and wounded Marines struck down in the dark continued to pool on the beaches.

By dawn, thousands of sandbags had been filled and the beginnings of order had been imposed on the topsy-turvy, shell-racked beachhead. The vital importance of the

(continued on page 101)

A view from the bridge of an LSM delivering fuel drums and rear-echelon troops to Iwo on D+1. Note the many amtracs working the beach and near shore. Once the combat assault was completed, amtracs were relegated to a logistical role. *Official USMC Photo*

Another fouled stretch of beach in the 4th Marine Division zone yields more evidence of a high D-day surf and brutal shelling on D-day and overnight. In the foreground is an abandoned amtrac, with its rear ramp down and a stalled jeep in its cargo bay. Another Japanese landing ship wrecked in the August 4 carrier raid can be seen in the center, and numerous inoperable landing craft, amtracs, and wheeled vehicles lie in between. *Official USMC Photo*

This view of Beach Red shows that heavy lifting gear has not yet been sent ashore here. Fuel drums must be manhandled inland from the surf line and stored temporarily in ad hoc open dumps like the one that is taking shape between the amtrac and the sandbagged bunker. The amtrac's marking indicates that it is assigned to Company B, 11th Amphibian Tractor Battalion. A large proportion of the beach party at this early juncture is provided by the five replacement drafts, which are already being broken up to provide combat fillers to front-line units. *Official USMC Photo*

If this stunt was being performed at some rear-area base, these Marines would undoubtedly be hauled off to a brig. But this is the war, and the ammo they are pitching around is urgently needed to keep the advance moving ahead. *Official USMC Photo*

A little way inland, on one of the 4th Division beaches, a shallow gully, possibly scooped out by a bulldozer, has been transformed into an ad hoc dump for expended brass casings from rounds fired by units of the 14th Marines. The valuable brass is saved, returned to the United States, and reused in new rounds. *Official USMC Photo*

Despite the high surf, LSMs line up to disgorge all manner of supplies and equipment. The weather is foul, and vehicles and smaller landing craft lay swamped in the surf, but the beach party carries on. *Official USMC Photo*

Every drop of the thousands and thousands of gallons of water required daily to sustain Marines on Iwo must be brought ashore until evaporators can be set up on the island. Much of the early supply of water was stowed in jerrycans at distant island bases, but ships and landing ships can produce enough with their onboard evaporators to sustain all the men who remain afloat as well as all who are ashore. But for now it must all be doled out at the rate of just 5 gallons per jerrycan. *Official USMC Photo*

Greatly aiding the dispersion of supplies and written messages was the new (to the Marine Corps) Weasel tracked amphibian jeep. The Weasel was initially designed for use in deep snow, not surf, but a hull that works in snow works in the water, and the Weasel was used for the most part amphibiously. *Official USMC Photo*

Marston Matting, also known as pierced steel planking, was designed as a ground stabilizer for airfields that needed to be built quickly and maintained under adverse weather conditions. Used with immense success, the matting became an essential component of the island-hopping campaign, which was defined by the quick placement of expeditionary airfields in places where natural materials such as rock or coral could not be found. At Iwo, the availability of Marston Matting was doubly important because the unstable volcanic ash that blanketed the invasion beaches would otherwise have choked the supply effort. By this late stage of the war, the matting panels have been prejoined on pallets to make deployment a truly simple and speedy evolution. The result is instant roadways that can be easily replaced as they become chewed up by heavy traffic. *Official USMC Photos*

Bulldozers got an early start on D+1 at scraping loose volcanic ash and sand down to the hard mantle beneath, then driving a fan of roadways inland from the beaches. The bulldozers also were used to haul palletloads of heavy goods along the earthen roadways. Note the engineering equipment at work in the center of the first photo and that, in the other, a line of laden amtracs and DUKWs is moving inland along a wide roadway directly after coming ashore. For all that much heavy equipment is gouging the land flat, the long line of Marines in the first photo is still manhandling heavy boxes inland to an expanding dump alongside the road. *Official USMC Photos*

A tank retriever (center) has towed half a dozen disabled 4th Tank Battalion Shermans from the surf or soft sand to firm ground overlooking the beach, and now crews and mechanics are readying them for a return to companies and platoons in combat to the north. *Official USMC Photo*

Heavy fighting inland and in the push out along the eastern shore ensures that Iwo Jima's major export on February 20 remains misery. *Official USMC Photos*

(continued from page 95)

orderly flow of supplies and men across well-ordered beaches cannot be minimized. The Marine Corps and the Pacific Fleet amphibious force had spent the entire Pacific War— and three earlier decades—preparing for an undertaking the size of Iwo Jima. Hard lessons along the way had been starkly and brutally direct, paid out in an ocean of blood at places such as Tarawa and Saipan. Make or break at Iwo hinged less on the fighting prowess of the front-line Marines than on the organizing capabilities and determination under fire of the logistician and shore laborer. Without the well-oiled machine required to deliver water on a waterless island, not to mention food and ammunition, and even morale-sustaining mail, the bravest of brave combatants could not possibly prevail.

Official USMC Photo

Official USMC Photos

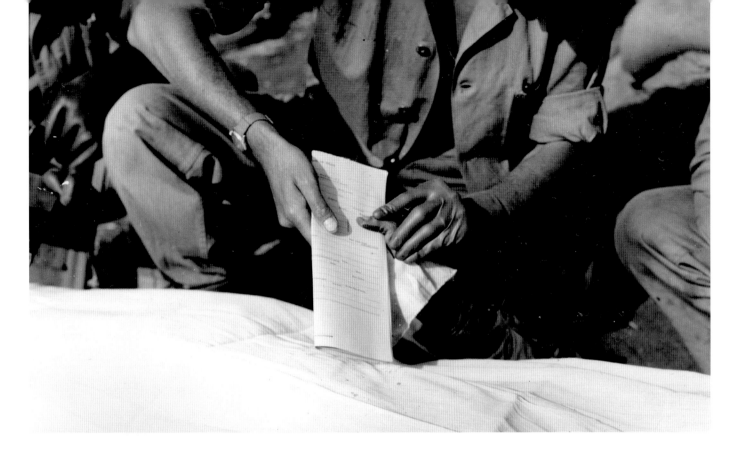

This grisly discovery was made in a cave behind Beach Blue-1. These Japanese appear to have been caught by a flamethrower. *Official USMC Photo*

CHAPTER 10

Suribachi

By dusk on D-day, the 5th Marine Division's 28th Marines had traversed from Beach Green, on the V Amphibious Corps extreme left flank, all the way across Iwo's narrow neck. By dawn on February 20, the regiment, composed in large part of former parachutists and some Raiders, faced in two directions: The battered 1st Battalion faced north in a blocking position, and 3/28 faced south, toward Mount Suribachi, the regimental objective. Until the 556-foot-high volcano was in Marine hands, the 28th Marines would fight a battle distinct from VAC's northward drive.

The terrain to the south of the 28th Marines line was largely open, strewn with large boulders thrown out by the volcano, impeded by gullies and folds, and guarded by hundreds of bunkers, pillboxes, and other fighting emplacements. Then there was the mountain itself, isolated, brooding, and completely dominant above the land approaches.

As other units of the 5th Marine Division arrived ashore, 1/28 was put into regimental reserve, and the rest of the regiment jumped off at 0830, with 2/28 on the right (west) and 3/28 on the left. The plan was to fully invest the base of the mountain to isolate the 1,600-man garrison and then attack uphill to the summit.

It was chilly and drizzling when the attack opened with a carrier strike that included napalm, bombs, and rockets, then a bombardment by Marine artillery (3/13), destroyers, and LCI(R)s. A designated destroyer to the west was placed at the direct disposal of gunfire coordinators with 2/28, and a minelayer to the east did the same for 3/28.

As soon as they stepped off, the Marines faced terrific fire from scores of emplacements, many heretofore silent, or at least uncharted. Guns rated up to 6 inches blasted the

A 28th Marines 81mm mortar fires on a target barring the way toward the base of Mount Suribachi. Note that the emplacement is defined by dirt-filled wooden boxes that are placed to hold back the liquidlike volcanic ash that covers this portion of Iwo Jima to a depth of several feet. *Official USMC Photo*

A carrier bomber pulls away after it bombs Japanese-held turf ahead of the 28th Marines' D+1 assault toward Mount Suribachi. In the foreground, a 37mm gunner from the regimental weapons company works to get his gun ready for the day's work.
Official USMC Photo

This 37mm gun crew fires on a target in support of 3/28's D+1 advance toward Mount Suribachi. The 37mm was designed as an antitank weapon, for which it did well enough against Japanese tanks, but its essential purpose in the Pacific evolved into an antiemplacement role. The versatile and highly portable 37mm was essentially a big rifle that could hit the same spot over and over to eventually punch a hole through concrete, logs, and even volcanic stone. In the defense, when it fired canister rounds, it served the role of a large shotgun. *Official USMC Photo*

attackers. Thanks to splendid observation from the heights, the gunnery was dead on. Eight 5th Tank Battalion Shermans behind the lines were harried from one place to another to yet another by spot-on fire as their crews attempted to transfer fuel and ammunition from damaged tanks.

Gains through the morning of D+1 were 50 to 70 yards. At 1100, the eight tanks were committed, and 37mm guns and 75mm halftracks were pushed forward to ranges down to pointblank. Close teamwork was required to destroy each emplacement in the

Closely coordinated antiemplacement attacks using combined arms and split-second timing were a significant feature of preassault training for Iwo Jima. The lessons behind the training had come at a high price over the course of the Pacific War. First, one or two flamethrower assaultmen directed their fire at one position, then infantrymen pelted the position with hand grenades and gunfire, and finally demolitions assaultmen blew up the emplacement with satchel charges. *Official USMC Photos*

Quite often, smoke and dust from demolitions charges and flamethrowers spread out from one emplacement to disclose the locations of numerous hidden entrances, caves, tunnels, and connected emplacements. *Official USMC Photo*

regiment's path. Typically, a flamethrower team worked forward with an infantry squad as a machine gun or other suppressive weapon reached for the embrasure to keep the defenders' heads down. When ready, the flamethrower operator (sometimes several) stepped up and fired several bursts. Then he stood aside as the infantrymen closed on the position to toss hand grenades. The infantry fired into the position through the embrasures, then perhaps a demolitions assault team worked forward to blow up the emplacement. When it was possible, flame tanks were used, or maybe 75mm halftracks.

By 1700, 2/28 and 3/28 had advanced about 200 yards at the cost of 29 killed and 133 wounded. Along the way the infantry and their supports killed at least 73 Japanese and blew up or otherwise neutralized approximately forty emplacements of all sizes and descriptions. The Marines also located and cut the main communications cable between the commander of the Suribachi defensive sector and General Kuribayashi's headquarters.

As night fell, the Japanese on Suribachi fired signal flares to request that artillery and mortar fire be placed on the attackers, who ended the day in positions well short of the base

Each Marine tank battalion fielded a full company of flame tanks, but these tended to be spread thin across an entire division's zone of operations. When a flame tank could be worked in against a target, the results were usually spectacular. *Official USMC Photo*

Private First Class Donald J. Ruhl of the
2d Battalion, 28th Marines.
Official USMC Photo

THE PRESIDENT OF THE UNITED STATES TAKES PRIDE IN PRESENTING
THE MEDAL OF HONOR POSTHUMOUSLY TO

PRIVATE FIRST CLASS DONALD J. RUHL
UNITED STATES MARINE CORPS RESERVE

FOR SERVICE AS SET FORTH IN THE FOLLOWING CITATION:

For conspicuous gallantry and intrepidity at the risk of his life above and beyond the call of duty while serving as a Rifleman in an Assault Platoon of Company E, 28th Marines, 5th Marine Division, in action against enemy Japanese Forces on Iwo Jima, Volcano Islands, from 19 to 21 February 1945. Quick to press the advantage after eight Japanese had been driven from a blockhouse on D-day, Private First Class Ruhl singlehandedly attacked the group, killing one of the enemy with his bayonet and another by rifle fire in his determined attempt to annihilate the escaping troops. Cool and undaunted as the fury of hostile resistance steadily increased throughout the night, he voluntarily left the shelter of his tank trap early in the morning of D-day plus 1 and moved out under tremendous volume of mortar and machine-gun fire to rescue a wounded Marine lying in an exposed position approximately forty yards forward of the line. Half pulling and half carrying the wounded man, he removed him to a defiladed position, called for an assistant and a stretcher and, again running the gantlet of hostile fire, carried the casualty to an aid station some three hundred yards distant on the beach. Returning to his platoon, he continued his valiant efforts, volunteering to investigate an apparently abandoned Japanese gun emplacement seventy-five yards forward of the flank during consolidation of the front lines, and subsequently occupying the position through the night to prevent the enemy from repossessing the valuable weapon. Pushing forward in the assault against the vast network of fortifications surrounding Mt. Suribachi the following morning, he crawled with his platoon guide to the top of a Japanese bunker to bring fire to bear on enemy troops located on the far side of the bunker. Suddenly a hostile grenade landed between the two Marines. Instantly Private First Class Ruhl called a warning to his fellow Marine and dived on the deadly missile, absorbing the full impact of the shattering explosion in his own body and protecting all within range from the danger of flying fragments although he might easily have dropped from his position on the edge of the bunker to the ground below. An indomitable fighter, Private First Class Ruhl rendered heroic service toward the defeat of a ruthless enemy, and his valor, initiative and unfaltering spirit of self-sacrifice in the face of almost certain death sustained and enhanced the highest traditions of the United States Naval Service. He gallantly gave his life for his country.

The morning of D+3 dawned wet, foggy, and miserable. Here, an officer manning an outpost in the lines of the 28th Marines attempts to locate targets or landmarks through the gloomy murk. *Official USMC Photo*

of the mountain. The request was met with an ongoing barrage as heavy as the one fired during the first night of the battle.

At dawn on D+2, which featured a cold rain and winds that threw up a 6-foot surf, the 28th Marines hunkered down as heavy preparatory fires screamed overhead against known emplacements and designated areas. Just before the scheduled 0825 resumption of the ground attack, 40 carrier fighters and bombers attacked to within a scary 100 yards of the infantry with guns, rockets, and bombs. The infantry, now including 1/28 in column of companies on the extreme left, jumped off on schedule, but without tank support, due to refueling problems. Naval gunfire was placed as needed ahead of the troops.

Gains were minimal with 75mm halftracks until 1100 hours, when 37mm guns and several rocket trucks were committed. As a result, 1/28 reached the base of the mountain at about noon.

The Japanese were quick to divine the extreme danger represented by the rocket launchers, and they took pains to single them out for counterfire. The rocketmen adapted quickly by withdrawing the trucks, which typically fired en masse while deployed hub-to-hub, then advancing them singly with only one man aboard to park, aim the launcher tubes, and press the firing buttons. Rockets are not a precise weapons system, which is why many tubes are

Marines from a light machine gun squad clean their weapons prior to commencing the advance on D+2. *Official USMC Photo*

The 28th Marines was supported throughout its advance on Mount Suribachi by the 105mm howitzers of 3/13. This howitzer, photographed on D+3, is set in well away from the shifting volcanic ash that hampered all manner of units closer to the invasion beaches. *Official USMC Photo*

A busy day at the office. This 28th Marines .30-caliber medium machine gun is spending most of D+3 in one place, hammering anything its crew can locate that might impede the final advance to the base of Mount Suribachi. *Official USMC Photo*

fired at once to flood an area that might be rich in targets. But they could administer a vicious beating when the area-saturation barrage was on the mark. It was tedious work, and often frustrating, but the powerful 4.5-inch rockets—a new weapon in the Marine arsenal—more than justified the extra effort.

In the regimental center, 3/28 hit an immovable barrier when it jumped off, but at-first-tiny inroads spread, and by 1100 the battalion was making strides. The first Japanese counterattack of the battle was beaten back, and then the thinned and perhaps demoralized opposition was more easily overcome. By 1400 3/28 had drawn abreast 1/28 at the base of Suribachi. On the far right, 2/28 was held to very small gains for most of the day in the face of unremitting heavy fire, but it eventually bulled through to join its sister battalions on a wide semicircle at the base of

the mountain. For gains ranging between 500 and 1,000 yards, the 28th Marines had given up 34 dead and 153 wounded—adding up with previous casualties to 25 percent losses in three days.

After the advance was halted, roving Marines poured gasoline into fissures from which they could hear voices and set the fuel ablaze to the accompaniment of screams and

Rockets were new to the Marine Corps bombardment capability, and only a provisional detachment was available for use at Iwo. Each truck could ripple off twenty-four 4.5-inch rockets in a matter of seconds and thus saturate a relatively small area with extremely deadly results. On the down side, as a rule the huge dust cloud blasted up by the rocket ignitions set the trucks up for quick, accurate counterbattery fire, so the rocketmen quickly developed elaborate fire-and-run tactics that were a perfect example of Darwinian principles. *Official USMC Photo*

Japanese discipline slipped somewhat on D+3 when the severely wounded commander of the Suribachi defensive sector decided in the absence of communication with the island commander to launch a counterattack. The attackers were mown down by Marines who, for the most part, had never seen Japanese soldiers in the open on Iwo Jima. *Official USMC Photo*

Supported by tanks, 3/28 attacks across open ground, all the way to the base of Mount Suribachi. *Official USMC Photo*

Marines assigned to the 5th Marine Division intelligence section erect a loadspeaker that will be used by a language officer to attempt to talk at least some of Suribachi's stubborn defenders into giving up. Captives were taken on and around the volcano. Some of them meekly surrendered, but it is not known how successful the direct appeal was in view of the iron discipline the broadcasts encouraged on the part of Japanese commanders and troop leaders. The majority of Japanese who surrendered on Iwo tended to be isolated from authority as well as suffering from hunger, thirst, or physical or emotional disabilities. *Official USMC Photo*

cooking-off ammunition. This was about as brutal as infantry warfare can get. The Japanese to the north once again contributed artillery and mortar fire that forced the Marine hunters to belay and find cover.

February 22 dawned miserable and rainy. Overnight the rain had turned the volcanic ash to mush that infiltrated the workings of many weapons, thus impeding the rate of fire the 28th Marines could put on the many targets that still lay to the front. The weather kept air support grounded on the carrier decks, and visibility from warships' gun directors was impaired. On the plus side, after two days of resupply fiascoes, seven fully fueled and armed Shermans were on hand at the front when the assault recommenced.

In the center, 3/28 lurched forward against Suribachi's north face, then dispatched a patrol eastward to the island's southern extremity. A patrol from 2/28 advanced to the same feature via a westward route, so the volcano was more or less surrounded. Most of the regiment spent the day dressing its lines and methodically taking out emplacements around the base—so much so that the defensive establishment was reduced to an estimated 300 survivors by nightfall. A sergeant from 3/28 returned from a lone-wolf foray partway up

Marine carrying parties on D+4 grab valuable supplies from an amtrac that has advanced all the way to the shadow of Mount Suribachi. *Official USMC Photo*

the northern slope to report no signs of the defenders. Even though this intimated an opportunity to take some ground quickly and cheaply, the regimental commander decided it was too late in the day for 3/28 to advance and then properly dig it in.

The assault on the volcano itself jumped off the next morning, D+4, February 23, 1945. There was only one practical route—up the north face—and so only 2/28 was designated to step off. The other two battalions scoured their zones for fighting emplacements they had thus far missed.

The first four Marines to move out of the 28th Marines lines, a patrol from Company F, did so at 0800. The four climbed all the way to the summit, where they encountered an unmanned machine gun strongpoint at the rim of the crater. A week of intense bombardment on these heights had made a tangle of blasted bunkers, pillboxes, and strewn weapons, gear, and supplies. There was no sign of a living being.

As always, provision has to be made to move the inevitable casualties from the front to aid stations behind the lines. In this case, on D+4, a seriously wounded Marine will be treated along the way by corpsmen aboard this dedicated evacuation amtrac. *Official USMC Photo*

CHAPTER 11

The Flag

At 0900 on D+4—Friday, February 23, 1945—while a four-man patrol from Company F, 2/28, was still reconnoitering a route to Suribachi's summit, the 2/28 commander, Lieutenant Colonel Chandler Johnson, sent off two three-man patrols, one each from Company D and Company F, to locate other possible routes. Next, Johnson assembled a much larger patrol with which he planned to send an American flag to the summit. Johnson designated the 24-man 3d Platoon of Company E, and the patrol leader was the company executive officer and former Marine Raider, 1st Lieutenant Harold George Schrier, who added fifteen men to the patrol as extra security. Before beginning the climb, Schrier led his men to the 2/28 command post for a pep talk from Lieutenant Colonel Johnson. As the patrol moved out, Johnson handed a folded American flag to George Schrier; it had been obtained from the transport USS *Missoula,* which had carried 2/28 to Iwo. At the command post, several hospital corpsmen and a Marine combat photographer attached themselves to the party, bringing the complement to 44.

The Schrier patrol made a rapid, surprisingly uneventful ascent. Somehow these Marines did not make contact with the first patrol to reach the summit; it descended and reported to the battalion command post without even seeing the Company E troops.

The battle-hardened Marines scoured the summit for Japanese who might put up a fight. Several looked for a way to get the flag up. One of the Marines spotted a Japanese soldier in a deep hole. He fired, the Japanese withdrew, and other Japanese threw grenades. The Marines peppered several cave mouths, and the skirmish ended.

As the base of the second flagpole is secured, Marines take down the first flag—the one their battalion commander feels is of transcendent historic importance. *Official USMC Photo by Private Robert R. Campbell*

The Schrier patrol has reached Suribachi's summit and reports that there is no sign of the enemy. Lieutenant Colonel Chandler Johnson orders Lieutenant George Schrier to raise the flag. Leatherneck *by Staff Sergeant Louis R. Lowery*

Marines affix the flag to a seven-foot iron pipe salvaged from a mountaintop cistern. Leatherneck *by Staff Sergeant Louis R. Lowery*

The Marines who had been looking for the means to raise the flag produced a 7-foot length of iron pipe they found in a mountaintop cistern. The flag was secured and raised upright without fanfare.

It was 1031. Below, all across the island and offshore, thousands of Americans fairly swooned as the national colors snapped fully open in the breeze. They had been watching the patrol's ascent for some time.

Staff Sergeant Lou Lowery, a twenty-four-year-old staff photographer for *Leatherneck* magazine, had braved the ascent for this moment. He snapped several photos, but he stopped when a Japanese soldier attacked from the mouth of a cave. A BARman cut down the intruder, but then a sword-wielding officer leaped into the battle. A Marine shot him dead with a .45-caliber automatic pistol, but then more grenades were hurled from cover. Staff Sergeant Lowery had to drop his camera and leap down the side of the mountain to avoid the bursting grenades, but other Marines opened fire on the caves, and a flamethrower team moved in to douse each one with flaming fuel.

Lou Lowery climbed back up to reclaim his camera. It was broken, but the exposed film was salvageable.

Members of the 3d Platoon, Company E, 2/28, work the national colors into a more secure stance. Leatherneck *by Staff Sergeant Louis R. Lowery*

The flag snapping in a brisk breeze was all but forgotten. Lieutenant Schrier's Marines turned to their real work, securing the summit and turning it into an observation post.

Down below, Lieutenant Colonel Johnson decided the flag was now too valuable to leave on Suribachi. He dispatched his adjutant's runner to find a replacement, climb the volcano, and substitute the new flag for its historic predecessor.

Others were drawn to the flag. One was the lieutenant who had led Company E's 3d Platoon until he had been wounded on the approaches to Suribachi. He went absent from the

Sergeant William Genaust, a thirty-eight-year-old combat photographer who had been recommended for a Navy Cross for gallantry on Saipan, filmed the second flag-raising in color with a standard-issue Filmo movie camera. These are stills selected from the movie film. Genaust was killed in early March when he came upon several live Japanese in a cave in northern Iwo Jima. *Official USMC Photos by Sergeant William Genaust*

The flag has only just been raised when it is rendered the honor of a hand salute by a pair of onlookers. *Official USMC Photo by Private Robert R. Campbell*

Opposite Page: "The Flag Raising at Iwo Jima" *National Archives & Records Administration by Joe Rosenthal*

Joe Rosenthal remains on his wobbly perch of stones as he takes his third and last photo atop Suribachi. Bill Genaust's hands and movie camera can be seen to the left of Rosenthal's feet. *Official USMC Photo by Private Robert R. Campbell*

hospital ship USS *Samaritan,* roped several Marines who had come down to report the morning's events to the 2/28 command post into going back, and limped to the summit to visit his men. Another Marine still photographer, Private Robert Campbell, joined the trek, as did a Marine movie cameraman, Sergeant William Genaust. Another sojourner was a myopic thirty-three-year-old civilian photographer, Joe Rosenthal, who had already accompanied Marines to Guam and Peleliu.

The photographers had joined forces and were about to leave the 2/28 command post to begin the ascent when a Marine with a flag under his arm arrived. He had talked the flag out of the possession of a navy ensign aboard *LST 779* as the vessel disgorged gear on the beach. Lieutenant Colonel Johnson turned the flag over to another Marine, who then joined up with the photographers.

The climb was arduous, especially for the diminutive Rosenthal, who was lugging a 150-pound pack. When they reached the summit, Rosenthal was especially winded.

The new flag, which was twice as big as the first, was lashed to another, longer, iron pipe. As this was going on, Joe Rosenthal frantically piled up some stones to stand on; he was 5-foot-5 and needed the advantage. Meanwhile, Campbell and Genaust photographed and filmed the proceedings. As the flag rose, Genaust stood a few feet to Rosenthal's left and was a little lower at eye level. Genaust's camera was loaded with color film and Rosenthal shot black-and-white. Rosenthal took one photo as the flag went up; he felt it was a bad shot, because the stones beneath his feet did not offer a solid base.

The first flag was lowered, and Campbell caught that moment. In fact, he took the only photo of both flags at one time.

As soon as the flag went up, three Marines pushed the foot of the pole deeper into the volcanic soil. Rosenthal shot that moment, too. Then more Marines rushed to get into a picture. Many raised their weapons and cheered. Rosenthal, still on his wobbly stones, took one shot of them while Campbell took a shot of Rosenthal taking that shot.

Joe Rosenthal's third and last photo atop Suribachi. This is the one he felt had a chance to be noticed. *National Archives & Records Administration by Joe Rosenthal*

Then the moment passed. Rosenthal had just three photos. Campbell had more, and Genaust had exposed several hundred feet of color film.

Rosenthal developed his own film aboard ship that night and dispatched the negatives to Guam via the daily press run by a navy seaplane. He was not especially impressed. He had missed the historic moment when the first flag went up, had huffed and puffed up the fierce mountain to photograph a substitution, and had pretty much botched the shot over a question of firm footing. Unbeknownst to Joe Rosenthal until he saw his flag-raising photo in print, a photo editor along the way cropped the original horizontal photo into a vertical image by focusing tightly on a solid pyramid of Marines beneath the rising national colors. What in the photographer's own mind had been an ordinary, rather pedestrian photo of little value had been turned into *The Photo*, an unsurpassed and unsurpassable masterpiece—immortal, emotional, fervent. The ultimate expression of American patriotism.

Guylines are brought in to prevent the flagpole and flag from being ripped from the ground by the heavy winds that prevail at Iwo's highest point. Then the Marines atop Suribachi scatter to get down to the job of protecting their nation's flag and neutralizing the Japanese who still occupy caves throughout the summit. *Official USMC Photos by Private Robert R. Campbell*

This view was taken within a day or two of the twin flag-raisings. The sentry who is standing post has a breathtaking view of the invasion beaches. Note that the guylines remain and that a cairn has been built up at the base of the flagpole to provide extra support. *Official USMC Photo*

Aftermath

Even as the drama atop Suribachi unfolded across the morning of D+4, elements of the 28th Marines along the line at the volcano's base took measures to ensure the security of the enterprise by bringing resistance in southern Iwo to an end. The main task was bunker hunting followed by bunker busting. Squads and platoons ventured forward to close the noose at the base entirely and advanced up the steep flanks to kill Japanese or seal

This is the vista that justifies the commitment of a reinforced infantry regiment to taking Suribachi—a perfect observation post from which nearly the entire battlefield can be viewed and plotted. The dust cloud from a large detonation can be seen directly over the head of the Marine at left.
Official USMC Photo

Joe Rosenthal. *Official USMC Photo by Private Robert R. Campbell*

them permanently into their demolished fortifications. Elements of the 5th Tank Battalion continued to support the 28th Marines, and elements of the 5th Engineer Battalion took control of the demolitions task.

For the most part, the Japanese went meekly to their deaths. Perhaps the knowledge that they had been abandoned to their fate, coupled with the mind-erasing effects of incessant heavy bombardment, not to mention their losing a spectacular battle so spectacularly, brought on this strange collective passivity. This is not to say that they all died quietly; many put up a fight, and American casualties rose.

Nightfall found George Schrier's patrol more or less on its own. All the "visiting firemen" had decamped, and no one sent reinforcements. About 45 men remained in control of the summit. They spread out and dug in, but the Japanese in bunkers all around them paid little attention and mounted no assaults. Farther down, an estimated 120 Japanese moved out as individuals or in small groups, left cover, and attempted to move northward. A few made it all the way to friendly lines—where they were lambasted as quitters—but most died in feeble little counterattacks or alone in the dark as they blundered into wary, wide-awake Marines. An

Marine infantrymen advance on D+4 to take an even firmer grip around the base of Mount Suribachi. Here, a bunker at ground level is blown and a 5th Tank Battalion Sherman raises its 75mm main gun to draw a bead on a possible target high on the volcano's northern face.
Official USMC Photo

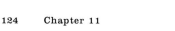

These Marines, sent partway up Suribachi on D+4, celebrate the capture of a reinforced concrete bunker by pausing briefly to display a captured flag. Note the Japanese machine gun behind the second Marine from the right. The bunker was undoubtedly the victim of at least one direct hit by a large-caliber naval gun. *Official USMC Photo*

Bunker busting became the order of the day following the flag raising. Here, smoke and dust billow from both ends of a tunnel that has been blown just below the summit. *Official USMC Photo*

These Japanese were among at least 120 who, during the night of February 23–24, attempted to escape the noose the 28th Marines had thrown around Suribachi or to sow chaos in the American rear. Thirty of the latter who attacked the 1/28 command post had to be beaten down by staff officers, headquarters troops, corpsmen, and a few sentries. *Official USMC Photo*

Near the volcano's summit and quite close to the flag, a demolition charge has been detonated to destroy a Japanese bunker directly overlooking the invasion beaches. *Official USMC Photo*

Even though the 28th Marines has occupied Suribachi's summit for a full day, D+5 at the base—and all the way up—was consumed by bunker-busting forays such as the one shown here. There were still hundreds of Japanese troops, including a large contingent of naval infantry, hunkered down beneath the volcano's honeycombed mantle, throughout the approaches, and all along the surrounding surf line. *Official USMC Photo*

Marines crowd around to witness that rarest of sights, a captured Japanese as he is being led from his hiding place atop Suribachi on D+5. *Official USMC Photo*

organized attempt by 30 Japanese to overrun the 1/28 command post failed miserably.

It was more of the same on D+5; the 28th Marines continued to hunt down surviving defenders and blow up their caves and hiding holes. A few dazed survivors were captured, but most of the defenders died. Hundreds were buried beneath the rubble or in little air pockets sealed all around, uncounted and uncountable.

In the end, the 5th Engineer Battalion certified the destruction of 165 concrete pillboxes and bunkers on Suribachi; the sealing of more than two hundred caves; and the detonation of thousands of artillery rounds, mines, grenades, and other explosive devices. While an accurate count was made impossible by the willful sealing of hundreds of living Japanese into caves and fighting emplacements, 1,231 Japanese corpses were counted on Suribachi alone.

When it was as over as it needed to be, the 28th Marines was placed in the 5th Marine Division reserve to rest, draw fresh gear, and take in replacements. To the north, the rest of V Amphibious Corps had been grinding forward from the beaches to secure D-day objectives, but the end of the battle was nowhere in sight.

A flamethrower is fired into a cave mouth. *Official USMC Photo*

CHAPTER 12

Up from the Beach

D+1

Suribachi was a necessary sideshow. The real battle was to the north, first for the two airfields and then for the high plateau beyond.

Dawn on D+1 found the better part of five Marine infantry regiments from two Marine divisions holding a very long double-curved line that was for the most part quite far from their D-day objectives. Of the fifteen infantry battalions ashore, only three at the extremities had come close to achieving their D-day land grab. On the far left, the 5th Marine Division's 3/28 and 1/28 had closed on the western beach but had not come close to smothering the defenses on Suribachi. On the far right, and despite heavy opposition, the 4th Marine Division's 3/25 anchored the V Amphibious Corps line at the East Boat Basin, only a few hundred yards short of its objective. The rest of the Marine line faced west rather than north, and the center battalions were far from capturing Airfield No. 1, much less investing about half of Airfield No. 2, as the plan had prescribed.

VAC and FMFPac took such a jaundiced view of the first day's shortfalls that they agreed to commit at least part of the VAC reserve—the veteran 3d Marine Division—as soon as possible. The division's transport flotilla, which arrived about 80 miles south of Iwo during the night, was alerted for a move to an offshore anchorage.

There was good news. About thirty thousand Marines had weathered the toughest challenge of an infinitely complex amphibious operation; they had gotten ashore in good order and had carved out a beachhead that seemed fairly secure against the obligatory night banzai attack the Japanese almost invariably mounted to throw invaders back into

A Company F, 2/27, platoon leader (with map) briefs his noncommissioned officers before continuing the attack on D+1. *Official USMC Photo*

In this sequence, a 5th Marine Division infantry unit is advancing over open ground when it comes under fire. The troops react by hitting the dirt, but soon they get up and rush forward toward their objective. Note in the third photo that the Marine at the far right, a radioman, is firing on a target. In the second photo, at left, he seems to be sparking the advance. *Official USMC Photos*

the sea. No such banzai had ever succeeded, and it was a proscribed tactic on Iwo, but even thirty thousand armed and aware Marines sweated it out that first night. While the beachhead was deemed secure against ground assault, the ferocious artillery assault that had opened a little after H-hour had not abated. Indeed, despite the many Japanese artillery pieces and mortars demolished during the day, it seemed to have become more intense. Infiltrators sowed mayhem in the rear and killed a few people, but their attacks were easily weathered.

Looking ahead at dawn on D+1, senior officers could see that D-day's shortfalls had nonetheless taken place over relatively smooth ground. Ahead lay broken, even jumbled, ground. The terrain ahead was going to be a nightmare. But it had to be taken, all of it.

From left to right, seven of the fifteen battalions available to the northward advance held a 4,000-yard line as follows: On the left, in the 5th Marine Division zone, 1/26 and 3/27; in the 4th Marine Division zone, 3/23, 2/24, 1/25, 2/25, and 3/25 bolstered by two companies of 1/24. Their first order of business would be to secure Airfield No. 1 and bring the entire line to a continuous northward facing.

A Marine movie cameraman captured this deadly sequence through a viewport in a 5th Tank Battalion Sherman. In the first three views, a Japanese soldier crawls for his life toward a low hummock. As he rounds the bend, a second Japanese pops his head up, and then one of them crawls back into view, where he is shot by the tank's bow machine gun. *Official USMC Photos*

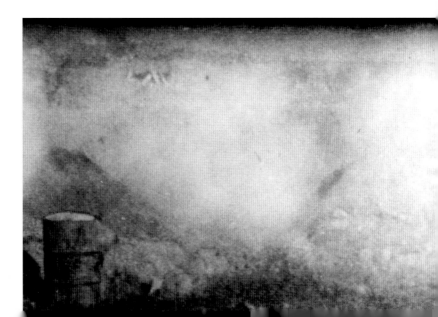

At 0500, an estimated five hundred Japanese forming up in the dark ahead of 1/23 were dispersed by artillery fire. On the debit side, Japanese artillery scored direct hits on the 2/25 command post, where the commanding officer, executive officer, and operations officer were all seriously wounded and a 4th Tank Battalion company commander was killed.

Units to the left had the farthest to travel to reach the first objective—the "O-1"—line. Following an intense preparatory bombardment, 1/26 and 3/27, strung out along a 1,000-yard front with 1/27 and 2/27 in reserve, mounted their assault at 0830. Both lead battalions immediately ran into dense defenses heavily augmented by continuous minefields and relentless artillery, mortar, and rocket support. Even bursting rounds from Japanese antiaircraft guns joined in the defense.

Yet the Marine infantry, supported by two Sherman tank companies and all manner of air and gunfire support, ground forward in the narrow 5th Division zone. By 1800 hours, the reinforced 27th Marines had conquered an average of 800 yards across the entire front. Adding to the dismay of not achieving its goals despite sustaining heavy casualties,

Private First Class Jacklyn H. Lucas of the 1st Battalion, 26th Marines.
Official USMC Photo

THE PRESIDENT OF THE UNITED STATES TAKES PRIDE IN PRESENTING THE MEDAL OF HONOR TO

PRIVATE FIRST CLASS JACKLYN H. LUCAS
UNITED STATES MARINE CORPS RESERVE

FOR SERVICE AS SET FORTH IN THE FOLLOWING CITATION:

For conspicuous gallantry and intrepidity at the risk of his life above and beyond the call of duty while serving with the 1st Battalion, 26th Marines, 5th Marine Division, during action against enemy Japanese forces on Iwo Jima, Volcano Islands, 20 February 1945. While creeping through a treacherous, twisting ravine which ran in close proximity to a fluid and uncertain front line on D-plus-1 day, Private First Class Lucas and three other men were suddenly ambushed by a hostile patrol which savagely attacked with rifle fire and grenades. Quick to act when the lives of the small group were endangered by two grenades which landed directly in front of them, Private First Class Lucas unhesitatingly hurled himself over his comrades upon one grenade and pulled the other one under him, absorbing the whole blasting force of the explosions in his own body in order to shield his companions from the concussion and murderous flying fragments. By his inspiring action and valiant spirit of self-sacrifice, he not only protected his comrades from certain injury or possible death, but also enabled them to rout the Japanese patrol and continue the advance. His exceptionally courageous initiative and loyalty reflect the highest credit upon Private First Class Lucas and the United States Naval Service.

The 24th Marines prepares to attack Airfield No. 1 at 0900 on D+1. This photo was taken 500 yards inland from Beach Yellow-2. *Official USMC Photo*

These 4th Marine Division scouts have reached Airfield No. 1's outer dispersal area and are peeking ahead under the cover of a wrecked Imperial Navy carrier bomber to locate Japanese snipers hiding out in other wrecked aircraft. *Official USMC Photo*

A unit of the 23d Marines infiltrates Airfield No. 1 on D+1. Note how close the edge of the airfield complex is to Beach Yellow-2. The Marines closest to the camera (center and far left) are moving in on two sides of a suspected pillbox. *Official USMC Photo*

A pair of 4th Division riflemen take a respite in the shadow of a wrecked truck to get their bearings and scout the terrain ahead. It doesn't take more than an hour or two of combat to make a wary veteran of any rifleman. *Official USMC Photo*

A Marine rifleman halts amid wreckage to draw a bead on something suspicious ahead while a wrecked 4th Tank Battalion Sherman stands as mute testimony that no one and nothing is immune to a well-placed—or just a lucky—shot. *Official USMC Photo*

the assault force was further sobered when 1/26 had to withdraw 200 yards to find decent defensive ground as proof against the perpetually predicted night banzai.

Closer to the center, the 4th Marine Division's 23d Marines, with 2/24 attached, jumped off aggressively at 0830 with pretty much the same support and the same response. Here, the Marines reached the northern end of Airfield No. 1 at about noon—and overran the edge of a Japanese defensive sector. Casualties were severe, but the reinforced 23d

Marines had a lot to show for them. There was less opposition on the ground the regiment attacked during the afternoon, but the terrain was more grueling and broken, so it was difficult to maintain a cohesive advance and the troops were confronted by heavier shellings. When the regiment was ordered to dig in that afternoon, it had advanced an average of 500 yards, faced north all along its front, and was in possession of most of Airfield No. 1.

On the V Amphibious Corps right, in the 25th Marines zone, the left-flank battalion, 1/25, had the farthest to go, while the center battalion, 2/25, only needed to take some high ground from which 1/25 could be supported by long-range fire. Hard hit on D-day, 3/25 was withdrawn from the line and replaced by all of 1/24.

Tank support in the 25th Marines zone was stymied by impossible terrain and a propensity of Japanese gunners to concentrate on the Shermans wherever they appeared. Enough artillery and mortar fire will eventually disable or destroy a tank, and it will certainly drive off the escorting infantry, which tankers absolutely require for eyes, ears, and close-in defense whenever the tanks' hatches are closed against shrapnel. So the tanks were neutralized, all that fire slowed or stopped the infantry, and brilliantly deployed machine guns putting out many thousands of bullets all across interlocking bands of fire were extremely difficult to take out when no one dared lift his head to

Sometimes there is no second-guessing luck. These unfortunate Marines took cover in a shellhole that received a direct hit by a Japanese artillery shell. *Official USMC Photo*

Amtracs laden with food, water, ammunition, and other necessities advance late on D+1 to replenish units of the 5th Marine Division. *Official USMC Photo*

A 105mm howitzer is hauled to a forward firing position by an engineer bulldozer. Artillery was usually towed by trucks, but the soft sand and jumbled terrain made movement by a powerful tracked vehicle a must. *Official USMC Photo*

locate them. The Japanese artillery also reached behind the front. At 1100, the 1/25 battalion aid station took a direct that killed six hospital corpsmen and wounded seven others. Throughout the day, the artillery also stymied efforts to get amtracs forward with loads of ammunition and water. To keep in the fight, the 25th Marines had to devote many troops to hauling supplies forward by hand.

At about 1600, Company B, 1/24, was strafed, bombed, and rocketed by carrier aircraft. A little later, before the stricken company had recovered, it was struck by two salvos from a cruiser's guns. The air strike killed five and wounded six, and the cruiser's guns left 1/24 with 90 casualties. At day's end, the bulk of 1/25 and 2/25 had advanced between 200 and 300 yards, but 1/25's left company had made almost no progress.

VAC now occupied a continuous 2-mile-wide line that ran pretty smoothly from shore to shore and fully took in Airfield No. 1. But the butcher's bill was unbelievable; Marines had never suffered so many losses in a single day. To get to this point in the advance north, the 5th Marine Division had lost about 1,500 Marines and corpsmen since landing, and the 4th Marine Division had lost approximately 2,000. To fans of butchers' bills, it can be said that 630 Japanese corpses were counted on the D+1 northern battlefields.

Hours earlier, as the day's reports only began to arrive at VAC headquarters, Major General Harry Schmidt ordered the 3d Marine Division to send the 21st Marines—veterans of Bougainville and Guam—ashore with its supports. These troops circled uselessly offshore for six hours as beach parties attempted to unfoul an adequate landing area in rising surf conditions. In the end, the fresh regimental combat team had to reboard its ships, an exhausting and perilous undertaking in even calm seas.

The same sea conditions brought one of the reserve artillery battalions to grief. At 1000, 3/14 began to land its 105mm howitzers in DUKWs on Yellow-1. It was tough going, thanks in part to heavy artillery fire, but the battalion made it ashore in decent order and fired its first missions at about 1730. Not so 4/14, which lost its first 105 moments after the DUKW it was in emerged into heavy seas from an LST and sank. Seven more howitzers, also aboard DUKWs, charged off the ramp despite the loss, all of them were swamped, and all

The Marine assault on D+2 was preceded by intense air, naval gunfire, and artillery concentrations all along the Japanese front and well into the rear. Shown here is a 155mm howitzer that has just fired. *Official USMC Photo*

This aerial view of part of a Marine 105mm battery shows how quickly the Marine artillerymen were able to organize themselves. Guns are fully protected by sandbags and natural barriers, crew shelters and ammunition storage are set, the fire direction center (left center) is fully functional, and a road has been pushed through. Note that the gun at the far right is crewed and firing. *Official USN Photo*

These 5th Division Marines, whose .30-caliber machine gun was damaged, have set up a captured Japanese Nambu-Hotchkiss medium machine gun to bolster the cover for advancing riflemen. *Official USMC Photo*

seven 105s were lost along with twelve gunners. Next, as the four remaining howitzer-carrying DUKWs neared the beach, two broached in the surf, losing their guns. The last two 105s remaining to 4/14 fired their first mission in the dark. To help bridge the shortfall in artillery support, VAC's 2d 155mm Howitzer Battalion sent a battery of four 155s ashore to the 5th Division zone, and these were hauled up an inland bluff by tractors and set in by 1840 hours.

D+2

Japanese troops attempted to mass in front of Marine lines in several places during the night of February 21–22, but they were driven off by artillery. Overall, the Marine artillery, bolstered by naval gunfire and LCI-borne 4.2-inch mortars, fired numerous harassment-and-interdiction and illumination missions throughout the Japanese rear. An attack by an estimated one hundred Japanese against 1/25 just before 0500 was easily defeated by combined arms.

Preparatory fires for the D+2 advance were provided by 33 Marine howitzers, 68 carrier fighters and bombers, 2 cruisers,

and a dozen destroyers. Both divisions jumped off at 0810 with the intention of reaching the O-1 line across Airfield No. 2.

D+2 brought more of the same against the determined and well-prepared foe. The 27th Marines, on the far left, was able to make good use of tanks even though it waded into an extremely dense mile-and-a-half-deep defensive sector in which as many as fifteen hundred caves, pillboxes, and bunkers would eventually be counted. Despite harrowing losses, the reinforced regiment advanced an average of 1,000 yards, nearly to the O-1 line.

Captain Robert H. Dunlap, the commanding officer of Company C, 1/26. *Official USMC Photo*

THE PRESIDENT OF THE UNITED STATES TAKES PRIDE IN PRESENTING THE MEDAL OF HONOR TO

CAPTAIN ROBERT H. DUNLAP

UNITED STATES MARINE CORPS RESERVE

FOR SERVICE AS SET FORTH IN THE FOLLOWING CITATION:

For conspicuous gallantry and intrepidity at the risk of his life above and beyond the call of duty as Commanding Officer of Company C, 1st Battalion, 26th Marines, 5th Marine Division, in action against enemy Japanese forces during the seizure of Iwo Jima in the Volcano Islands, on 20 and 21 February 1945. Defying uninterrupted blasts of Japanese artillery, mortar, rifle and machine-gun fire, Captain Dunlap led his troops in a determined advance from low ground uphill toward the steep cliffs from which the enemy poured a devastating rain of shrapnel and bullets, steadily inching forward until the tremendous volume of enemy fire from the caves located high to his front temporarily halted his progress. Determined not to yield, he crawled alone approximately 200 yards forward of his front lines, took observation at the base of the cliff 50 yards from Japanese lines, located the enemy gun position and returned to his own lines where he relayed the vital information to supporting artillery and naval gunfire units. Persistently disregarding his own personal safety, he placed himself in an exposed vantage point to direct more accurately the supporting fire and, working without respite for two days and two nights under constant enemy fire, skillfully directed a smashing bombardment against the almost impregnable Japanese positions despite numerous obstacles and heavy Marine casualties. A brilliant leader, Captain Dunlap inspired his men to heroic efforts during this critical phase of the battle and by his cool decision, indomitable fighting spirit and daring tactics in the face of fanatic opposition greatly accelerated the final decisive defeat of Japanese countermeasures in his sector and materially furthered the continued advance of his company. His great personal valor and gallant spirit of self-sacrifice throughout the bitter hostilities reflect the highest credit upon Captain Dunlap and the United States Naval Service.

Next inland was the 4th Marine Division's reinforced 23d Marines, which attacked in two waves 600 yards apart—and gained all of a hundred yards in return for a very high casualty rate.

The 25th Marines and 1/24 attacked with three battalions abreast, 3/25 in reserve, and two companies of the 4th Tank Battalion performing yeoman service. A furious assault

THE PRESIDENT OF THE UNITED STATES TAKES PRIDE IN PRESENTING THE MEDAL OF HONOR TO

CAPTAIN JOSEPH J. MCCARTHY
UNITED STATES MARINE CORPS RESERVE

FOR SERVICE AS SET FORTH IN THE FOLLOWING CITATION:

For conspicuous gallantry and intrepidity at the risk of his life above and beyond the call of duty as Commanding Officer of Company G, 2d Battalion, 24th Marines, 4th Marine Division, in action against enemy Japanese forces during the seizure of Iwo Jima, Volcano Islands, on 21 February 1945. Determined to break through the enemy's cross-island defenses, Captain McCarthy acted on his own initiative when his company advance was held up by uninterrupted Japanese rifle, machine-gun and high velocity 47mm fire during the approach to Motoyama Airfield No. 2. Quickly organizing a demolitions and flamethrower team to accompany his picked rifle squad, he fearlessly led the way across 75 yards of fire-swept ground, charged a heavily fortified pillbox on the ridge to the front and, personally hurling hand grenades into the emplacement as he directed the combined operations of his small assault group, completely destroyed the hostile installation. Spotting two Japanese soldiers attempting an escape from the shattered pillbox, he boldly stood upright in full view of the enemy and dispatched both troops before advancing to a second emplacement under greatly intensified fire and blasted the strong fortifications with a well-planned demolitions attack. Subsequently entering the ruins, he found a Japanese taking aim at one of his men and with alert presence of mind jumped the enemy, disarmed and shot him with his own weapon. Then, intent on smashing through the narrow breach, he rallied the remainder of his company and pressed a full attack with furious aggressiveness until he had neutralized all resistance and captured the ridge. An inspiring leader and indomitable fighter, Captain McCarthy consistently disregarded all personal danger during the fierce conflict and by his brilliant professional skill, daring tactics and tenacious perseverance in the face of overwhelming odds, contributed materially to the success of his division's operations against this savagely defended outpost of the Japanese Empire. His cool decision and outstanding valor reflect the highest credit upon Captain McCarthy and enhance the finest traditions of the United States Naval Service.

Captain Joseph J. McCarthy, commanding officer of Company G, 2/24. *Official USMC Photo*

by 1/24, bolstered by tanks and dense fire from 1/14, drove the defenders forward to The Quarry and adjacent high ground. The 1/25 commander was killed by artillery fire in the morning. The capture of the high ground on the coast opened other opportunities inland

Sergeant Ross F. Gray of Company A, 1/25. *Official USMC Photo*

THE PRESIDENT OF THE UNITED STATES TAKES PRIDE IN PRESENTING
THE MEDAL OF HONOR TO

SERGEANT ROSS F. GRAY
UNITED STATES MARINE CORPS RESERVE

FOR SERVICE AS SET FORTH IN THE FOLLOWING CITATION:

For conspicuous gallantry and intrepidity at the risk of his life above and beyond the call of duty as Acting Platoon Sergeant serving with Company A, 1st Battalion, 25th Marines, 4th Marine Division, in action against enemy Japanese forces on Iwo Jima, Volcano Islands, 21 February 1945. Shrewdly gauging the tactical situation when his platoon was held up by a sudden barrage of hostile grenades while advancing toward the high ground northeast of Airfield No. 1, Sergeant Gray promptly organized the withdrawal of his men from enemy grenade range, quickly moved forward alone to reconnoiter and discovered a heavily mined area extending along the front of a strong network of emplacements joined by covered communication trenches. Although assailed by furious gunfire, he cleared a path leading through the minefield to one of the fortifications then returned to the platoon position and, informing his leader of the serious situation, volunteered to initiate an attack while being covered by three fellow Marines. Alone and unarmed but carrying a 24-pound satchel charge, he crept up the Japanese emplacement, boldly hurled the short-fused explosive and sealed the entrance. Instantly taken under machine-gun fire from a second entrance to the same position, he unhesitatingly braved the increasingly vicious fusillades to crawl back for another charge, returned to his objective and blasted the second opening, thereby demolishing the position. Repeatedly covering the ground between the savagely defended enemy fortifications and his platoon area, he systematically approached, attacked and withdrew under blanketing fire to destroy a total of six Japanese positions, more than twenty-five of the enemy and a quantity of vital ordnance gear and ammunition. Stouthearted and indomitable, Sergeant Gray had single-handedly overcome a strong enemy garrison and had completely disarmed a large mine field before finally rejoining his unit and, by his great personal valor, daring tactics and tenacious perseverance in the face of extreme peril, had contributed materially to the fulfillment of his company's mission. His gallant conduct throughout enhanced and sustained the highest traditions of the United States Naval Service.

The Marine at the front of this small group of bunker busters breaks cover to check the route ahead. To the left, a flamethrower assaultman awaits the call to advance, as does the bazookaman to the right (the muzzle of the bazooka is just noticeable beneath the barrel of his .30-caliber carbine). *Official USMC Photo*

that took the regimental left forward an average of 300 yards, but the right gained only 50 yards, which threatened to unbalance the line. In the afternoon, 3/25 was ordered to close a gap that had been widening between 1/25 and 2/25, but it was tough, tough going. Another late-developing gap at the juncture of the two divisions caused 1/27 to be committed to seal it, but the 5th Division right and the 4th Division left remained about 400 yards apart.

Day-long, carrier air provided about eight hundred support sorties, and land-based artillery was bolstered by two cruisers, eleven destroyers, and two sections of LCIs firing 4.2-inch mortars.

The 21st Marines was finally landed in good order and dispatched to join the 4th Marine Division the next day for the drive on Airfield No. 2. Airfield No. 1 was securely in American hands, but Seabees were unable to get even a tiny stretch of runway into shape, as hoped, for OY spotter planes. The 4th Marine Division forward command post landed in the afternoon under command of the assistant division commander, but the division commander and the rear command post remained afloat.

D+2 ended with twelve battered infantry battalions on line facing the Japanese, and the fresh 21st Marines standing by near Airfield No. 1 to relieve the 23d Marines as soon as possible. Casualties ashore now exceeded 4,500, and the 4th Marine Division reported that it was at 68 percent of its authorized combat strength. To add to everything, a cold drizzle trending toward a real downpour started in the night and exhausted, emotionally drained—and now drenched and chilled—infantrymen stayed awake in anticipation of the standard banzai. Instead, the invasion fleet was attacked.

This Marine engineer is checking an improvised cave-busting device he will no doubt employ on D+2. Blocks of explosives have been taped to a board at the end of a long pole. The objective is to insert the charge through the mouth of a cave and lever it up against one side so it cannot be shoved back out by the cave's occupants. This is an old trick first used by Marine parachutists at Gavutu on the opening day of the 1942 Guadalcanal campaign. *Official USMC Photo*

A battalion of the 23d Marines forms up on a vast stretch of open ground before moving into the line on D+2. Note tanks on the horizon that will spearhead the assault and amtracs (center left) that are resupplying the troops. *Official USMC Photo*

Between approximately 1645 and 2030 a stream composed of an estimated fifty kamikaze aircraft originating from airfields around Tokyo penetrated the carrier-based combat air patrol to attack U.S. Navy vessels off Iwo. The fleet carrier USS *Saratoga*, embarking a night air group, was struck by three kamikazes and a bomb shortly after 1700, then by another bomb at about 1846. Losses were 123 killed or

Even though the horrors of bottomless volcanic ash have been left behind on the beach, this Sherman has dug itself into soft sand while supporting the D+2 advance far from the shore. Note here that thick boards have been fixed over the tank's side armor. This is a universal deterrent this late in the war against Japanese magnetic antitank grenades. The sandbags serve the same purpose, as do the spare tracks clipped to the turret. Less common are the spikes that have been affixed to the hatches to deter suicidal Japanese who might try to pry them open, a common occurrence in earlier island campaigns going back to Guadalcanal. *Official USMC Photo*

These Marines have managed to find some foliage in which to hunker down on the approaches to Airfield No. 2 *Official USMC Photo*

This is a posed photo of a 4th Marine Division fire team: two riflemen equipped with M-1 Garand .30-caliber semiautomatic rifles and, in the middle, an automatic rifleman equipped with a Browning Automatic Rifle (BAR). These three have chucked their light field packs, and the rifleman with the hand grenade has set his web belt on the parapet of their temporary fighting hole. He has no leggings on, but his teammates do. Both of the riflemen have fixed bayonets to their M-1s. *Official USMC Photo*

A wounded 4th Marine Division 81mm mortar crewman is manhandled from the gun pit near Beach Yellow after being wounded on D+2 by Japanese counterbattery fire. It is a truism that if you can hit them, they can hit you. *Official USMC Photo*

Behind the lines, a 5th Engineer Battalion assault squad built around a flamethrower advances warily on a pillbox that *might* have been defanged by advancing infantry. *Official USMC Photo*

missing and 192 wounded, plus 42 precious night fighters and night bombers lost in fires or in water landings. The escort carrier USS *Lunga Point* was slightly damaged at about 1830 hours, and at 1900 hours the escort carrier USS *Bismarck Sea* was dealt a mortal blow that resulted in uncontrollable fires leading to a massive explosion that killed 318 of her complement of 943 crew and airmen. Also hit were an LST that sustained no losses and a cargo ship on which 17 were killed and 44 were wounded. All of the attackers were lost, most to fierce antiaircraft fire.

A dead Japanese soldier. A passing Marine has marked the spot with the dead man's bayoneted rifle to help clean-up crews locate the body for eventual burial or cremation—purely a sanitation measure. *Official USMC Photo*

At the end of another long day buttoned up in their tanks (and a tank retriever), and after they have completed refueling and rearming, Sherman crews dismount for food and rest. Each crew was composed of five men: the tank commander, gunner, loader, driver, and bow machine gunner. *Official USMC Photo*

D+3

Ashore, the night of February 21–22 was more of the same, plus a bombing attack thrown in during the kamikaze surge. In the morning there was heavy rain and deep mud made abrasive by volcano dust and sand. The average distance the Marine front was on D+3 from the O-1 line—the D-day objective—was 1,200 yards. Combat fatigue—as emotional collapse under fire was then known—was becoming a problem that had to be dealt with. Morale was falling. The 21st Marines relieved the 23d Marines and 2/24 (except for two 81mm mortar platoons) in place in the VAC center, and the 26th Marines replaced the 27th Marines (except attached 1/26) on the VAC left when it attacked through the latter's line.

Ahead of the 26th Marines was a long bluff that ran northeast to southwest inland from the west coast until it curved west across the front near Airfield No. 2. So, in addition to merely formidable defenses, the regiment now

The front-line troops lived like warrior monks, taking sustenance and tiny doses of pleasure as and where they could. *Official USMC Photo*

This amtrac, which is critically needed to haul supplies and evacuate the wounded, has been damaged badly enough on D+2 to require surgery. Next to it is a shot-up Japanese warplane. Note the amtrac's extended cleats, which were designed to propel it through water. *Official USMC Photo*

Major General Keller Rockey's 5th Marine Division forward command post landed in the morning on D+2 and spent most of the day getting set up ashore. The rear command post ran the division throughout the day from aboard ship. General Rockey is seen here with the handset to his ear. *Official USMC Photo*

Even as late as D+2, a drowned tank is still in the pothole that bilged it on D-day, and wrecked gear is still strewn at the water line. *Official USMC Photo*

This wounded Marine enjoys a smoke and a nice bed of life preservers aboard a coast guard LCVP on its way to a hospital ship. *Official U.S. Coast Guard Photo*

This 20mm gun crew aboard an LST offshore Iwo Jima is faced with two kamikazes at once as the leading edge of the Tokyo-based attack reaches the fleet at dusk on D+2. *Official USN Photo*

Early on D+3, a 1/26 BAR man breaks cover to brave enemy fire in a solitary rush toward the battalion's objective. *Official USMC Photo*

Despite rough seas, the kamikaze attack, and a steep gangway, these wounded Americans will shortly receive the best medical care their nation can provide. *Official USMC Photo*

In his rush over fire-swept open ground near Airfield No. 2, this BAR man from Company G, 3/26, is undeterred by the corpse of a Marine who failed in his effort to reach cover ahead. That's what it takes to win battles, thousands of times over. *Official USMC Photo*

This 5th Division Marine was shot dead while humping ammunition and communications wire to a front-line position. *Official USMC Photo*

faced formidable *elevated* defenses with great vistas. The assault by all three battalions in line stepped off at 0835, following an intense preparatory barrage. It immediately drew heavy fire of all types from the heights, not to mention artillery and mortars. At 0940, the 3/26 commander and executive officer were killed by a mortar round, but that did not stall an advance that ultimately stopped 400 yards north of where it had begun.

The 21st Marines sent 1/21 and 2/21 into the attack (and held 3/21 in reserve) as soon as its relief of the 23d Marines was completed. The ridge facing the 27th Marines lay

This 5th Division front-line forward observer is under fire as he calls for artillery to be placed on a Japanese mortar position that is holding up the advance between the western beach and Airfield No. 2. *Official USMC Photo*

This 105mm howitzer is dug into a revetted position and set to fire a mission in support of the D+2 advance. At top right, infantry replacements march forward to join the fight. Brass shell casings are saved to be returned to armories in the States for reuse. *Official USMC Photo*

These Marines from Company G, 2/24, including the 60mm mortar squad in the foreground, appear to be at the end of their ropes physically and psychologically. Yet, as they rest a bit in a gully beside a damaged Sherman, they know they are only minutes away from being recommitted to the fight to conquer ground between the airfields. The Marine in the foreground looking directly into the camera has an authentic thousand-yard stare. By this point, still less than four days into the battle, Company G has sustained 40 percent losses on Iwo Jima. *Official USMC Photo*

A tremendous explosion has been triggered by a routine assault on a Japanese pillbox. Most likely the demolitions charge reached an underground ammunition storage dump. *Official USMC Photo*

Marines at a front-line command post dug into the debris-strewn battlefield use a battalion-level radio to call in a fire-support mission. *Official USMC Photo*

At least five Marine rocket trucks each let loose a salvo of 24 4.5-inch rockets to support the Marine advance. *Official USMC Photo*

THE PRESIDENT OF THE UNITED STATES TAKES PRIDE IN PRESENTING
THE MEDAL OF HONOR TO

COLONEL JUSTICE M. CHAMBERS
UNITED STATES MARINE CORPS RESERVE

FOR SERVICE AS SET FORTH IN THE FOLLOWING CITATION:

For conspicuous gallantry and intrepidity at the risk of his life above and beyond the call of duty as Commanding Officer of the 3d Assault Battalion Landing Team, 25th Marines, 4th Marine Division, in action against enemy Japanese forces on Iwo Jima, Volcano Islands from 19 to 22 February 1945. Under a furious barrage of enemy machine-gun and small-arms fire from the commanding cliffs on the right, Colonel Chambers, then Lieutenant Colonel, landed immediately after the initial assault waves of his Battalion on D-day to find the momentum of the assault threatened by heavy casualties from withering Japanese artillery, mortar, rocket, machine-gun and rifle fire. Exposed to relentless hostile fire, he coolly reorganized his battle-weary men, inspiring them to heroic efforts by his own valor and leading them in an attack on the critical, impregnable high ground from which the enemy was pouring an increasing volume of fire directly onto troops ashore as well as amphibious craft in succeeding waves. Constantly in the front lines encouraging his men to push forward against the enemy's savage resistance, Colonel Chambers led the 8-hour battle to carry the flanking ridge top and reduce the enemy's fields of aimed fire, thus protecting the vital foothold gained. In constant defiance of hostile fire while reconnoitering the entire Regimental Combat Team zone of action, he maintained contact with adjacent units and forwarded vital information to the Regimental Commander. His zealous fighting spirit undiminished despite terrific casualties and the loss of most of his key officers, he again reorganized his troops for renewed attack against the enemy's main line of resistance and was directing the fire of the rocket platoon when he fell, critically wounded. Evacuated under heavy Japanese fire, Colonel Chambers, by forceful leadership, courage and fortitude in the face of staggering odds, was directly instrumental in ensuring the success of subsequent operations of the V Amphibious Corps on Iwo Jima, thereby sustaining and enhancing the finest traditions of the United States Naval Service.

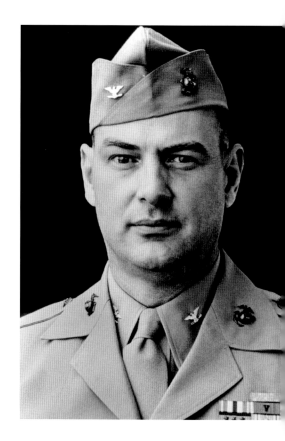

Colonel Justice M. Chambers, the commanding officer of 3/25. The Silver Star ribbon "Jumpin' Joe" Chambers wears was earned at Tulagi in August 1942, when he was first wounded in action while commanding a company of Marine Raiders. *Official USMC Photo*

ahead, uphill in the rain, and the defense was intricate and stubborn. The wide open spaces of the Airfield No. 2 taxiways denied cover and had to be sidestepped, but the area between taxiways and runways was defended in depth and could not be ignored. By the time they stopped, 2/21 had gained 250 yards at one spot and less elsewhere, and 1/21 had advanced all of 50 yards. The 1/21 commander had been wounded by a mortar round. When the

The Japanese fielded rocket launchers, as seen here, capable of firing 200mm projectiles. *Official USMC Photos*

A Japanese light machine gunner and two infantrymen who died in the open. The machine gun is a 6.5mm Nambu, a very reliable and lethal weapon. *Official USMC Photos*

These Marines have dug deeper into a gully during a break in the assault to avoid incessant Japanese mortar fire. The Marine in the foreground is asleep. *Official USMC Photo*

The original caption for this photo reads, "Nip and Tuck – Battlewise Marines use a sling made of enemy leggings to remove bodies from the entrance of a dugout on Iwo. The Leathernecks know from past experience that the Japs may be playing possum." *Official USMC Photo*

This Marine took off his gear during a break in the cover of a shellhole, but he was killed by Japanese fire. *Official USMC Photo*

Sergeant Hershel W. Williams, a demolitions assaultman serving with 1/21. *Official USMC Photo*

A tank crewman passes a 75mm round through the gunner's hatch during a break in the fighting. Note that a barrier against magnetic antitank grenades has been built over the wheels as well as over the side of the crew compartment. *Official USMC Photo*

21st Marines halted there was a wide gap to the left, so the battered 26th Marines—which had already deemed its new line too exposed to fire—gave up all of its D+3 gains.

The inability of the 21st Marines to advance meant that the 25th Marines and 1/24 could not safely take new ground. For all that, 1/25 was able to keep pace with 1/21, on its left, and gained about 200 yards in all. But 2/25, 3/25, and 1/24 advanced not at all, though 3/25 was able to coax the release of some rocket trucks to its sector, and they blanketed a hill 800 yards to the front with their lethal, mind-altering barrage. Retaliatory fire wounded the 3/25 commander, Lieutenant Colonel Justice Chambers, as he directed the rocket fire from a front-line observation post.

After dark on February 22, Task Force 58 sailed north to strike the Tokyo area, leaving only a night carrier and her escorts. This departure would be noticed right away in the amount of air and gunfire support available for on-call response. On the other hand, the headquarters of the 9th Naval Construction Brigade had set up ashore during the day and thus the building program involving infrastructure and Airfield No. 1 received a huge shot in the arm.

The night continued rainy and harrowing. A Japanese night attack on the left drove in 1/26's outposts, and Japanese swimmers attempted—but failed—to infiltrate the 5th

Burial at sea. Even though the 4th and 5th Marine divisions had opened cemeteries ashore, wounded soldiers of the sea who died aboard ship were committed to the deep.
Official USMC Photo

Marine Division rear. Also, an attempt at 0500 by a hundred Japanese to infiltrate between 2/25 and 3/25 was defeated.

D+4

No Marine ground unit had reached the O-1 line yet, but the VAC D+4 objective was the O-2 line, well beyond Airfield No. 2. This must have been a ploy to keep the troops pumped up, but it was a weak ploy. The troops were quite capable of seeing that two vital factors were working against them. If it was possible, the Japanese defenses were on better ground and far denser than they had been to this point. The front-line Marines were beyond tired, and their nerves were jagged. Moreover, the high rate of casualties, especially among senior officers and trusted troop leaders, was nearing an unsustainable level. Many, many good men had given their all for the crappy gains to date—well short of every pessimistic projection.

But at 0730 on D+4—February 23, 1945—every Marine who was asked and still could resumed the northward grind. Warships and warplanes helped them, as did the battered tank battalions and all manner of land-based supporting arms. But that's all the good all that steel could do—*help* the infantry; it couldn't do their job for them.

The Marine center pushed and pushed hard toward the high ground, but no amount of pushing did the trick; gains were nil. The only progress was at the margins: on the far right, the 24th Marines advanced 300 yards along the beach; on the far left, the 26th Marines and 2/27 fought forward about 200 yards, but they could not find a way to defend the new front line, so they withdrew. Japanese artillery severely wounded the 2/26 commander.

Machine gunners from 2/27 haul their carts forward as infantrymen hold tight beside a track bordering Airfield No. 2. Despite mortar fire and snipers who are staked out all along this section of the 5th Marine Division front, these troops will step off into the attack as soon as the .30-caliber medium machine guns can put out fire to keep Japanese heads down. Some of the infantrymen are relaxing, while others compulsively rearrange their gear. *Official USMC Photos*

A Company G, 26th Marines, Thompson submachine gunner searches for targets along the route he will soon have to take toward Airfield No. 2. The .45-caliber Thompson, a beautifully machined weapon, was notoriously inaccurate at even medium range, but it was lethal at short range. *Official USMC Photo*

Marines from 3/26 scale one of uncountable rock-strewn slopes fronting Airfield No. 2 during a direct frontal assault. The Japanese took full advantage of the natural jumble to blend in everything from one-man spider holes to pillboxes to caves to immense multi-story bunkers that often could not be seen even after the troops manning them had opened fire. No doubt, beyond this slope is another one, scrupulously defended to the last man. *Official USMC Photo*

A Sherman from Company C, 5th Tank Battalion, has moved to the fore to sweep ground destined for an infantry assault with solid armor-piercing rounds in case the target is an emplacement or high-explosives rounds if it finds Japanese troops in the open or if the gunner sees nothing much of any targets. Spotted or not, there are plenty of targets out there. *Official USMC Photo*

A 5th Division Marine runs ahead for all he is worth as he leads an assault on a Japanese dugout that is holding things up near Airfield No. 2. As sure as there are Japanese dug in ahead, there are Marines willing to give their all to dislodge and kill them. *Official USMC Photo*

Light machine gunners from Company H, 27th Marines, crowd into a small gully to evade fire from a Japanese machine gun to their front. Ahead to their right, a lone flamethrower assaultman also is hugging the ground to adjust his tanks. At the top of this photo might be a concrete structure whose camouflage has been blown off, indicating that these Marines might be nearly on top of an otherwise beautifully camouflaged bunker. *Official USMC Photo*

This highly lethal Japanese 47mm antitank gun was camouflaged and sited down a roadway before it fell to Marine infantry. In addition to antitank units organic to infantry commands, the Japanese deployed five independent antitank battalions on Iwo. *Official USMC Photo*

Rain or shine, hell or high water, Marine artillery stands shoulder-to-shoulder with Marine infantry. This 105mm howitzer crew belongs to the 4th Marine Division's 14th Marines. *Official USMC Photo*

The Marines had no way of knowing yet that they had pushed up against the forward edge of the most formidable defensive zone on the island and that they now faced General Kuribayashi's best-trained troops, the veteran 145th Infantry Regiment. The defenses were anchored at both shores on high ground, and the vast flat area represented in the middle by Airfield No. 2 afforded superb fields of fire for the many lethal 47mm antitank guns dug in there, with fields of fire converging on every inch of the coverless runways. Mines and booby traps abounded, and every square inch was registered in by Kuribayashi's crippled but nonetheless powerful artillery, mortar, and rocket supports.

A day's fighting saw 1/21 stymied at its line of departure. There were some gains in the 2/21 sector as far as the approaches to the southwest taxiway, but a surge across the northeast-southwest runway was driven back by the 47mms and machine guns.

Weapons at the ready, a pair of Marine riflemen are in the open to make sure that Japanese here are in fact dead. In the center background of this view, a Marine flamethrower team, also mopping up, fires into a cave mouth. *Official USMC Photo*

Two 5th Tank Battalion gun tanks pass a blade tank as they move northward to spearhead yet another attempt to bull through to occupy all of Airfield No. 2 on D+4. *Official USMC Photo*

This Japanese soldier, was pulled to the surface after his fighting emplacement was torched.
Official USMC Photo

A troop leader with Company L, 3/21, has just moved to the front south of Airfield No. 2 after relieving 4th Marine Division troops on the firing line. There is a good chance this Marine is a veteran of Guam, and perhaps even Bougainville, but Iwo is going to teach him a whole new course on combat lethality. *Official USMC Photo*

A developing ammunition shortage was set straight on D+4 when new beaches on the west side of the island were established and the eastern landing beaches were pretty much unfouled. Use of beaches on both sides of Iwo now allowed for greater flexibility if the wind was adverse on one shore or the other. And more beaches made it easier to

This Japanese soldier, killed near Airfield No. 2, was a victim of Company F, 2/21, on that unit's first day in the battle for Iwo. *Official USMC Photo*

Marines from 2/23 seek shelter from mortar fire on D+4 exactly in the same place in the Airfield No. 1 dispersal area as a Marine dueled with a sniper on D+1 (see page 134). The damaged tank seen in the earlier photo has not yet been recovered. *Official USMC Photo*

Marines double-check a cave that has been blown by advancing troops. Note the detonation cord on the ground and, directly behind the Marine on the right, the hilt of a Japanese sword whose blade has been run into the ground. *Official USMC Photo*

The new 4th Marine Division command post hosts an open-air meeting of the top brass. Left to right are: Major General Clifton Cates, 4th Division commanding general; Major General Harry Schmidt, VAC commanding general; Lieutenant General Holland Smith, FMFPac commanding general; and Brigadier General Franklin Hart, 4th Division assistant commander. *Official USMC Photo*

This 21st Marines light machine gun has been set up beside a road connecting Airfield No. 1 with Airfield No. 2, ahead. An overturned Sherman tank can be seen immediately to the right of the machine gun's barrel. *Official USMC Photo*

Here, 3d Medical Battalion doctors, corpsmen, and medical service personnel man a busy front-line casualty clearing station in a concrete personnel shelter beside Airfield No. 1.
Official USMC Photo

accommodate the commitment of the 21st Marines to the battle—not to mention the possibility of more 3d Marine Division units coming ashore.

Major General Harry Schmidt ventured ashore on D+4 to view the front and confer with his division commanders. Schmidt's subordinates suggested that the O-2 line was too far ahead to be a reasonable next objective, and in the end they agreed to a modified line in which the beach objectives remained fixed while, in the center, an area slightly north of Airfield No. 2 was made the objective. This gave the line regiments something tangible and obvious to work toward.

When a newsman asked Harry Schmidt if he felt the preinvasion schedule—victory in ten days—would hold, Schmidt said he had no idea why not. Schmidt must have known

The stream of casualties seemed endless.
Official USMC Photos

how blustery that sounded, but his troops had made some real headway so far, even if the next phase of the campaign might be grueling and costly (as if it hadn't already been both). One thing was certain: the portions of Iwo in Marine hands would remain in Marine hands, no question. There were no reinforcements in General Kuribayashi's future, and it is questionable that, even if he changed his defense theory, he might strike a serious enough blow in the open with the troops he had left. Mayhem, yes, but certainly not victory. On February 23, the battle for Iwo became what Kuribayashi had always dreamed it would be, a battle of attrition, no more, no less.

By D+4 the large number of casualties threatened to overwhelm the 4th and 5th Marine division troops assigned to bury the dead in the two newly opened division cemeteries. The dead Americans in this photo, who have been recovered from the beaches and battlefields all the way to the front or have succumbed to their wounds in aid stations ashore, must be sprayed with disinfectants to help prevent the spread of disease. *Official USMC Photo*

CHAPTER 13

All the Comforts

The strategic goal of the invasion of Iwo Jima was the airfields. Airfield No.1 was in American hands by sunset on D+1, but it was still targeted by Japanese guns, mortars, and rockets. As well, bypassed emplacements and strongpoints needed to be located and reduced to rubble and ash. Nevertheless, as the fighting front moved north, Airfield No. 1 became increasingly secure and workable. Marine engineers were for the most part consigned to the assault or to help mop up and seal bypassed fighting positions or clear mines. Navy Seabees took on the rehabilitation of useful Japanese facilities and the construction of roads, dumps, and beach improvements. The Seabee units assigned to airfield rehabilitation took casualties from Japanese shells and rockets fired to impede their progress.

On February 24—D+5—Major General Harry Schmidt brought his VAC command post ashore. Major General Graves Erskine, the 3d Marine Division commanding general, also moved ashore with his forward command post, but no fresh combat units from his division landed to join the reinforced 21st Marines even though Erskine was given a formal sector to oversee in the VAC center; it consisted pretty much of Airfield No. 2. A seaplane base also was designated on D+5 for courier and long-range search aircraft.

On D+6, the 3d Marine Division's reinforced 9th Marines landed and went right into battle on Airfield No. 2. Thanks to the incredibly efficient and hardworking Seabees, Airfield No. 1 was declared secure for emergency landings. As soon as that was announced, a Navy FM fighter from one of the escort carriers declared an emergency and landed. So did a clutch of Marine Observation Squadron 4 (VMO-4) OY observation planes, which immediately got to work spotting targets for Marine artillery.

The first mail from home reached Iwo on February 27, flown in by a PBM reconnaissance bomber from Guam. It made all the difference in the world to some Marines. *Official USMC Photo*

Shown here is a divisional ration dump. After the shock and hyperactivity of simply landing on Iwo had worn off, the beachhead was organized for maximum efficiency for the landing, stowage, and movement of supplies. More or less permanent encampments were established, complete with troop and equipment shelters, and the dumps themselves were squared away among a network of roadways that allowed for rapid ingress, unloading and loading, and egress. All this was in conformity with the many hard lessons learned all across the wide Pacific. *Official USMC Photo*

Marines fight a fire in an ammunition dump. Note the many African-American Marines in this photo. For the most part, they served with segregated supply units, especially Marine ammunition companies that accompanied invasion forces as corps service troops.
Official USMC Photo

The 3d Marine Division commander, Major General Graves Erskine (center, with map), landed on February 24 to establish his division forward command post beside Airfield No. 1.
Official USMC Photo

Seabees rush to complete enough work on Airfield No. 1 to get it operational as soon as possible. *Official USMC Photo*

On D+7, the first detachment of navy PBM twin-engine patrol bombers arrived at the Iwo seaplane base to begin long-range searches for Japanese ships, especially sub-marines. An army antiaircraft battalion landed on D+7, and its first assignment was to use its 90mm guns to shell two islets off the west coast from which mortars and rockets were fired sporadically on 5th

A Marine bomb-disposal team working beside Airfield No. 1 gingerly raises a Japanese 550-pound bomb to the bed of a specially rigged truck so it can be driven to a safe spot for detonation. *Official USMC Photo*

Navy Lieutenant Noah Butt lifts his FM carrier fighter off Airfield No. 1 after making some minor history by becoming the first pilot to land on the hard-won runway. *Official USMC Photo*

One of the first two Marine OY spotter planes based ashore refuels on Airfield No. 1. The divisional observation squadrons performed vital work even before they could use the airfield because several LSTs had been specially equipped with gear that could launch and recover the light planes. This OY, *Estabrook Nightingale*, was purchased by funds raised by the Estabrook School of Detroit, Michigan. This was typical at this late stage of the war, right on up to cruisers that were funded via donations from the cities for which they were named. *Official USMC Photo*

A U.S. Navy Martin PBM reconnaissance bomber taxies close to a ship from which it will receive a consignment of film and news stories turned in by military correspondents. This PBM, which is equipped with jet auxiliary boosters, will fly to Guam, and the news materials will then be flown to Hawaii and on to the mainland. Other PBMs were permanently based off Iwo to provide long-range reconnaissance on the lookout for Japanese submarines and surface warships. *Official USN Photo*

An army 90mm antiaircraft gun is dug in near Airfield No. 1 on February 26, 1945. *Official USMC Photo*

Mail from home. *Official USMC Photo*

Marine Division troops. Farther out, aircraft from the antisubmarine warfare escort carrier USS *Anzio* sank an Imperial Navy coastal submarine off Chichi Jima, and a U.S. Navy destroyer sank a fleet submarine carrying three manned suicide torpedoes.

On D+8, seaplanes brought in the first mail and whole blood, the latter direct from San Francisco packed in ice, and the navy's Evacuation Hospital No. 1—the first unit of its kind on its first deployment—set up on Beach Purple on the west coast. An army field hospital and the 4th Marine Division hospital also took in their first patients this day, and

February 27 was marked by the opening of several field hospitals ashore, which greatly reduced the time wounded Marines had to wait for definitive treatment. The first whole blood reached the island on February 27, packed in ice aboard a PBM that started its journey in San Francisco. *Official USMC Photo*

On February 28, three Army Air Forces long-range air transports out of Saipan dropped urgently needed medical supplies and spare parts on Iwo. Airfield No. 1 was not quite ready to host heavy airplanes, but the February 28 trip was predicated on the fact that the transports could have set down if they had to. *Official USMC Photo*

Another type of specialist who rooted through the rear in search of bypassed Japanese was the linguist, who could try to talk them into surrendering. The 4th Marine Division linguist leaning against the mouth of this bypassed cave is not armed, but the men behind him to his left have their pistols drawn. If the occupants of the cave refuse to surrender, or if there's nobody home, the cave will be permanently sealed with explosives. If no linguist is available to try to talk a cave's occupants into giving up, combat engineers will go straight to Plan B. *Official USMC Photo*

Mopping up the rear took patience and special skills, including nonhuman perceptions. Marine war dogs and their handlers accompanied search teams that combed the rear for bypassed Japanese holding out in isolated caves and fighting emplacements. Each division fielded its own war dog platoon. This 5th Division team of handler and war dog checks through an abandoned Japanese barracks area on February 27. *Official USMC Photo*

It became easier during the second week of fighting to find Japanese willing to surrender. Many turned out to be Okinawan or Korean labor conscripts (i.e., slaves) with little use for Japanese warrior values, but Japanese combatants also started to give up. Many were wounded, sick, starving, or thirsty, but others were not, and more of the healthy ones were first-line troops who simply no longer saw the point of dying for a lost cause. Having had no training whatsoever in resisting interrogation, the average Japanese prisoner of war usually spilled every detail he knew about the defenses he had been manning and the condition of the troops with whom he had served. *Official USMC Photo*

Official USMC Photos

the army's post-invasion garrison command and an advance detachment of the Army Air Forces' VII Fighter Command also landed, as did the first VMO-5 OYs. Aircraft from the USS *Anzio* sank an Imperial Navy submarine carrying three manned suicide torpedoes, thus ending the Imperial Navy submarine force's last sally.

On D+9—the last day of February—the VAC and 4th and 5th division hospitals were able to handle full patient loads, and four LST hospital ships completely filled with wounded were ordered to sail for Saipan. During the day, three Army Air Forces transports based on Saipan air-dropped 5 tons of medical supplies and vitally needed spare parts (including three bundles that had to be recovered from the sea). In the evening, the lower half of Iwo was sprayed with DDT by a pair of carrier-based TBMs.

During the night, Iwo's naval command post received the news that no more effort would be made to support the defenders because it had become obvious that the Americans were about to invade Okinawa, which was much closer to home.

CHAPTER 14

Grinding Forward

The sad fact about the battle for Iwo Jima was that it was going to remain every bit as difficult a slugfest as it had been on the first four days of the V Amphibious Corps drive to the north, D+1 to D+4. There would be no magic bullets, no smooth ploys, no sudden collapse. If victory was to be attained on Iwo, it would be cumulative (which is to say attritional) and extremely expensive—more expensive by far than any other real-estate transfer in the Pacific War.

Only one combination of tactics would suffice: straight-ahead frontal attacks. There were no quiet flanks or gaps from which an assault could be deftly uncoiled to the defenders' surprise and dismay. There were no gaps or vacuums in the enemy lines that didn't have to be carved out at great cost; any given sector a thousand yards by a thousand yards might contain an aggregate of four or five hundred carefully and redundantly sited defensive emplacements, all stone or *thick* reinforced concrete, featuring multiple interlocking bands of fire and serviced by steady, well-trained troops who could move from any one to many others below the surface, or at least in defilade, without being perceived in any way until they opened fire.

The Japanese knew what they were about. The loss of key leaders or especially gallant, show-the-way officers and noncommissioned officers did not diminish the effectiveness of the defense in the same way such losses hurt the offense; all the Japanese had to do—and they all knew it—was go where they had been trained (or last ordered) to go and defend either unto death or until told to go elsewhere.

But as "luck" always has it in a stolid, stoic, straight-up, toe-to-toe slugfest, opportunities tend to favor the side that can see better and react quicker. The Japanese were no

Marines under fire in the rain keep their heads down as a Sherman advances up a road while firing its 75mm main gun. The rifleman in the foreground keeps rain from the barrel by placing a prophylactic over the opening—a common trick of the trade. *Official USMC Photo*

Light machine gunners from Company L, 3/21, prepare to move out to take Airfield No. 2. A full-strength light machine gun squad consists of five men. The others might be outside the view, but it is also possible that only two members remain. *Official USMC Photo*

A 3/21 flame gunner stands tall to take out a cave or emplacement just over the crest of this rise. Without flamethrower assaultmen willing to take enormous gambles, the advance on Iwo would have bogged down at the beach. Casualties among such men were frightful. *Official USMC Photo*

One reason why flamethrower assaultmen were willing to go forward with their bulky gear was that the Marine riflemen they worked with were willing to take precisely the same risks to support them. These Marines from 3/21 have located a cave entrance atop a rock-strewn hill overlooking Airfield No. 2. *Official USMC Photo*

The willingness of tank crews to advance with the infantry was also crucial and just as symbiotic. Here, 4th Marine Division riflemen cover a 4th Tank Battalion blade tank, and vice versa. *Official USMC Photo*

A 4th Marine Division .30-caliber medium machine gun is deployed to cover the front during a lull in the advance. The water-cooled mediums and their heavy ammunition were difficult to move up alongside infantry during an advance, but they were leapfrogged forward to anchor even a temporary defensive line. In an attack, they were employed to suppress Japanese fire while infantrymen advanced. *Official USMC Photo*

For all that they looked impregnable, Shermans were vulnerable to all sorts of mischief. In this case, a 3d Tank Battalion Sherman's drive wheel has fallen prey to a mine. Fortunately, most damaged tanks could be rehabilitated in the field. *Official USMC Photo*

There were no hot meals to be had on the Marine front lines, but there was plenty of food carried as close to the front as possible by the versatile amtracs. *Official USMC Photo*

This medium machine gun squad is apparently under fire as it builds up its defenses in the shadow of a high Japanese-held hill. *Official USMC Photo*

This is what sudden death looks like without quite being death. The 105mm round was fired by a 14th Marines howitzer on February 24. *Official USMC Photo*

A major advance of the period was the erection of salt water evaporators ashore, which made it much easier to get drinking water to many thousands of troops and support personnel. Each evaporator shown here could desalinate 250 gallons per hour. *Official USMC Photo*

slouches in the brains department, and they were no more fated to die, per se, than the Americans were fated to win, but they had no way to move heavy guns and no access to outside help. Their numbers and resources were immense—but finite. And static. If there had been a long break in the battle so the Americans could bring in reinforcements from afar, the Japanese would have been able to exploit the respite in only minimal fashion. Every battle opportunity afforded the Japanese could eventually be reversed if the Americans were willing to pay the toll in ever more gallons of blood. No scenario except a complete loss of faith by the Americans could make the inevitable outcome less inevitable. Of course, General Kuribayashi's siren song, whose words were about imposing a complete loss of faith, was exactly what the Japanese defensive principles were built around. But if you need to know whether Americans even contemplated such an outcome, it must be said that the American commanders and the American troops ended the D+4 fight feeling that their offensive was at last kicking into high gear, that they had found the rhythm, and that the percussion section was at last poised to kick some serious ass. In other words, it was

Fresh water was stored and transported in 5-gallon jerrycans that could be easily carried to troops at the front. By February 23, the Japanese were running out of water and would soon be placed on an unsustainable water ration—if they could get water at all. Marines had no such problem, except temporarily from time to time at the forwardmost front. Most Marines carried several canteens that were replenished daily, and the tropical island campaigns of the earlier years of the Pacific War had made water-rationing discipline a top training priority. *Official USMC Photo*

The casualties kept coming with no end in sight. *Official USMC Photo*

Artillery and naval gunfire observers call targets during the battle for Airfield No. 2. *Official USMC Photo*

On February 25, the 3d Marine Division's veteran 9th Marines advances across Airfield No. 1 to begin its maiden assault on Iwo. By the end of the day, the regiment and attached units will occupy nearly all of Airfield No. 2—but not the commanding heights to the north. *Official USMC Photo*

sad, true, and not overly discouraging that nearly 7,800 casualties (including 1,605 killed) had been expended to learn exactly how to defeat Kuribayashi's best-laid plan.

There was a palpable electricity in the air that fifth night ashore; the battered remnants of front-line Marines tasted victory and would not have gone back even if the notion of going back had occurred to them. Out ahead, intertwined with blood and suffering, lay only victory. It was each Marine's goal to live a long and prosperous life after victory, but, short of that, it was each Marine's goal to help every defender reach his goal, which was to die for the emperor. "Not going back" had directly opposite meanings for Americans and Japanese in the Pacific War. The difference why one side left its sons dead on island after island and why the other knew beyond a doubt that losing was not going to happen to them.

Scenes of battle. *Official USMC Photos*

Scenes of battle. *Official USMC Photos*

This Marine infantry company command group was lucky to find cover in a Japanese concrete emplacement during a fierce bombardment, but . . .

. . . the fuel tanks being carried forward by this flamethrower team took a direct hit. *Official USMC Photos*

Note the deep, bloodless wound on this Marine's left shoulder blade. Probably he was struck by hot shrapnel that cauterized the wound. He is biting his tongue to deal with the pain. *Official USMC Photo*

A large-caliber round explodes next to a 5th Tank Battalion Sherman returning from a run along the west coast. Note that the turret is aimed backward, toward the enemy. *Official USMC Photo*

D+5

In fighting on February 24, VAC moved steadily but slowly and expensively toward the intermediate O-A objective line, some 800 yards north of Airfield No. 2 between the O-1 and O-2 objective lines. This was initially easier and less costly to do on both flanks than by the 21st Marines, in the center, because the center was the dead-flat Airfield No. 2, and it was dominated by an especially well-conceived defense-in-depth on high ground. The reentrant in the center of the Marine line was eliminated on D+5, but there was no getting up the high ground.

D+6

On February 25, nearly all of Airfield No. 2 ended up in Marine hands, but "secured" is no way to categorize it; the area was still dominated by plunging fire from high ground, which the Marines could not take despite repeated gallant assaults that killed or maimed plenty of gallant Marines—now from the fresh 9th Marine Regiment, which mounted its maiden Iwo Jima assault through the bleeding 21st Marines. On the left, the 5th Marine Division's only front-line regiment, the 26th, stood down to wait for the adjacent 3d Marine Division to come abreast its D+5 gains. On the right, the 4th Marine Division's 24th Marines advanced far enough to secure the eastern end of Airfield No. 2's east-west runway; then it stopped to wait for the 9th Marines to draw abreast.

A Marine rifleman, then a litter team, sprint past a dead Japanese soldier. Japanese machine-gun fire is clipping branches from the tree they are passing. *Official USMC Photos*

A Company E, 2/9, platoon leader lays out the plan of attack to his men as they prepare to mop up intensely defended ground on the verges of Airfield No. 2. *Official USMC Photo*

This smiling Marine knows that he has sustained a million-dollar wound—a ticket home that is not serious enough to maim him. For all that, he might have a change of heart. Hundreds of Marines returned to their units after having their wounds treated, many without authorization from the doctors. *Official USMC Photo*

In this breathtaking view, a Company E, 2/9, flamethrower assaultman leaps from cover to cross open ground on his way to a pillbox that is holding up his unit's advance. *Official USMC Photo*

This 3d Tank Battalion crewman is being treated in the Company G, 2/9, aid station after his Sherman was hit by Japanese fire. *Official USMC Photo*

Inevitably, in every frontal assault, the casualties persisted. Here, 2/9 stretcher bearers rush the driver of a Weasel to an aid station after the vehicle took a direct hit while carrying vitally needed supplies to the front lines. *Official USMC Photo*

Over Tokyo that night, XXI Bomber Command ran its first incendiary raid and proved that fire bombs dropped on a Japanese city at night were better for the war effort than bombing precision targets such as aircraft factories during the day. Also, Task Force 58 carrier aircraft pummeled Tokyo at the start of a two-day visit.

D+7

On February 26, VAC continued to grind forward toward the O-A line, but the opposition faced in the center by the 9th Marines didn't slacken a bit despite an immense effort by artillery to stun the Japanese by the ferocity of its bombardment. On the right, the 4th Marine Division reached Hill 382, another swatch of densely defended high ground that could be mounted and taken only by direct frontal assault. The 5th Division made only

No Japanese fire mission went unanswered, and Marines were covered every step of the way across Iwo with all manner of support. Here, a Marine infantry company 60mm mortar squad has set up in a former Japanese machine-gun position well suited to this use. *Official USMC Photo*

Two views of deadly Hill 382, which at first fell to the 4th Marine Division without much of a fight, then stymied Marines for several days after they voluntarily gave it up. Marine movie cameraman Sergeant Bill Genaust, who shot the flag raising on Suribachi on February 23, was killed in a cave on Hill 382. All facets of the hill were covered by scores of Japanese fighting positions accessed by an impressive complex of caves and chutes through which defenders could be shuttled vertically and laterally. Every cave mouth had to be sealed with explosives to slowly close off the entire system. *Official USMC Photos*

February 26 went down in the history books as a quiet day in the 5th Marine Division zone, so the division could wait for units to the right to catch up. Nevertheless, opportunities to advance could not be ignored. Here, at 0850, Company F, 2/26, opens a local advance over open ground.
Official USMC Photo

At 0900, Company F is still advancing across open ground. The troops are under fire, but they continue to move on their objective. *Official USMC Photo*

The tank retrievers were increasingly busy as the battle wore on. The tanks were the first things Japanese gunners fired at whenever they appeared at the front, mines claimed many by blowing off treads, unseen pitfalls claimed others, and general wear and tear and cumulative damage added to the toll. Most tanks could be adequately patched and sent back into action, but fewer and fewer Shermans were available over time.
Official USMC Photo

A Japanese artillery round scores a direct hit on a 5th Tank Battalion Sherman. The highly flammable gasoline-fueled medium tanks looked much safer than they were. *Official USMC Photo*

When the Japanese garrison's last water storage fell into the hands of 5th Division Marines on February 26, about a hundred Japanese charged to their deaths in bright moonlight in an ill-conceived effort to regain the vital resource. *Official USMC Photo*

Light machine gunners lay down suppressive fire as the February 27 assaults begin. *Official USMC Photo*

Several Marines race up a rock-strewn slope to try to get over a ridge line as Japanese rifle and machine-gun fire reach out to them from several sides. *Official USMC Photo*

limited advances on the VAC left to keep from getting ahead of the other divisions. That evening, between rain showers, an estimated company of Japanese attempted to advance down the west coast to recapture five cisterns—the last Japanese water reserve—that had been taken by Marines during the day. The attack never really got under way before the Japanese were brushed aside beneath bright moonlight by artillery and naval gunfire.

This 3d Division Marine was killed inside a shell crater as he tried to affix his bayonet to his rifle. *Official USMC Photo*

A Marine fire team waits its turn to advance while other Marines pass through on their way to the rear. *Official USMC Photo*

Stalled by fire, several Marines on this slope attempt to locate the Japanese guns by peeking over the crest of the slope. *Official USMC Photo*

A Marine acting platoon leader has just been shot in the face by a sharp-eyed Japanese soldier while peering around a corner to reconnoiter the enemy-held terrain ahead. *Official USMC Photo*

Bayonet fixed and ready to dive to cover, this front-line Marine nevertheless grunts his way through a tangle of underbrush toward the top of his rocky objective. *Official USMC Photo*

A 3d Marine Division flamethrower assaultman and his assistant have just been killed by a mortar round while taking cover in a deep bomb crater. *Official USMC Photo*

Walking wounded. There is a good chance that these Marines, who exhibit no bandages and look like they might be crying, are "combat fatigue" casualties. The longer the battle went on, the more of them there were. Combat fatigue, also called "war neurosis" at the time, was as legitimate and debilitating as a gunshot wound, and it struck men of all ages, ranks, and life experience. *Official USMC Photo*

The stream of casualties never abated. *Official USMC Photo*

D+8

On February 27, the 9th Marines finally gained enough traction to drive over the heights dominating Airfield No. 2. The 23d Marines, in the 4th Division zone, bounded to the top of Hill 382, but a gap on the regimental left could be closed only through a voluntary withdrawal. On the division and corps far right, the 25th Marines made gains on the coast but was stalled before a heavily defended pocket fronting Minami. The 5th Marine Division replaced the 26th Marines with the 27th, and that regiment made measured gains on the VAC left.

Marine engineers probe the taxiway connecting Airfield No. 1 with Airfield No. 2 for buried mines. This is the first step toward rehabilitating Iwo's hard-won central runway complex. *Official USMC Photo*

D+9

On February 28, with the O-2 line "only" a few hundred yards ahead of its front-line regiments, VAC raised its planning sights to the O-3 line, which contemplated the capture of uncompleted Airfield No. 3. In the center, where the strongest effort was to be made, the somewhat rested 21st Marines attacked through the 9th Marines behind a

(continued on page 196)

THE PRESIDENT OF THE UNITED STATES TAKES PRIDE IN PRESENTING
THE MEDAL OF HONOR TO

PRIVATE FIRST CLASS DOUGLAS T. JACOBSON
UNITED STATES MARINE CORPS RESERVE

FOR SERVICE AS SET FORTH IN THE FOLLOWING CITATION:

For conspicuous gallantry and intrepidity at the risk of his life above and beyond the call of duty while serving with the 3d Battalion, 23d Marines, 4th Marine Division, in combat against enemy Japanese forces during the seizure of Iwo Jima in the Volcano Islands, 26 February 1945. Promptly destroying a stubborn 20mm antiaircraft gun and its crew after assuming the duties of a bazooka man who had been killed, Private First Class Jacobson waged a relentless battle as his unit fought desperately toward the summit of Hill 382 in an effort to penetrate the heart of Japanese cross-island defenses. Employing his weapon with ready accuracy when his platoon was halted by overwhelming enemy fire on 26 February, he first destroyed two hostile machine-gun positions, then attacked a large blockhouse, completely neutralizing the fortification before dispatching the five-man crew of a pillbox and exploding the installation with a terrific demolitions blast. Moving steadily forward, he wiped out an earth-covered rifle emplacement and, confronted by a cluster of similar emplacements which constituted the perimeter of enemy defenses in his assigned sector, fearlessly advanced, quickly reduced all six positions to a shambles, killed ten of the enemy and enabled our forces to occupy the strongpoint. Determined to widen the breach thus forced, he volunteered his services to an adjacent assault company, neutralized a pillbox holding up its advance, opened fire on a Japanese tank pouring a steady stream of bullets on one of our supporting tanks and smashed the enemy tank's gun turret in a brief but furious action culminating in a single-handed assault against still another blockhouse and the subsequent neutralization of its firepower. By his dauntless skill and valor, Private First Class Jacobson destroyed a total of sixteen enemy positions and annihilated approximately seventy-five Japanese, thereby contributing essentially to the success of his division's operations against the fanatically defended outpost of the Japanese Empire. His gallant conduct in the face of tremendous odds enhanced and sustained the highest traditions of the United States Naval Service.

Private First Class Douglas T. Jacobson of 3/23. *Official USMC Photo*

At a relatively safe supply point between the central and southern airfields, a 9th Marines flamethrower assaultman replenishes the fuel and air tanks of his deadly weapon from pressurized cylinders. *Official USMC Photo*

A 3/12 105mm howitzer fires on a target beyond the 3d Marine Division's fighting front north of Airfield No. 2. Every available howitzer in the regiment has a job to do—taking out emplacements just ahead of the infantry, or reaching out against Japanese guns supporting their own troops. *Official USMC Photo*

This 24th Marines fire team has found a more than ample supply of wood for their cook fire as they settle down for a hot meal and some needed rest on the afternoon of February 27. *Official USMC Photo*

This Marine was shot dead as he tried to find cover in a shallow depression on a flat plain with no secure cover to offer. *Official USMC Photo*

Private Wilson D. Watson of 2/9.
Official USMC Photo

A pair of Shermans move on Japanese emplacements on the outskirts of Airfield No. 2. Barely perceptible between the tanks is a hole several Marines are using to evade Japanese machine-gun fire.
Official USMC Photo

THE PRESIDENT OF THE UNITED STATES TAKES PRIDE IN PRESENTING

THE MEDAL OF HONOR POSTHUMOUSLY TO

GUNNERY SERGEANT WILLIAM C. WALSH

UNITED STATES MARINE CORPS RESERVE

FOR SERVICE AS SET FORTH IN THE FOLLOWING CITATION:

For conspicuous gallantry and intrepidity at the risk of his life above and beyond the call of duty as Leader of an Assault Platoon, serving with Company G, 3d Battalion, 27th Marines, 5th Marine Division, in action against enemy Japanese forces at Iwo Jima, Volcano Islands, on 27 February 1945. With the advance of his company toward Hill 362 disrupted by vicious machine-gun fire from a forward position which guarded the approaches to this key enemy stronghold, Gunnery Sergeant Walsh fearlessly charged at the head of his platoon against the Japanese entrenched on the ridge above him, utterly oblivious to the unrelenting fury of hostile automatic weapons and hand grenades employed with fanatic desperation to smash his daring assault. Thrown back by the enemy's savage resistance, he once again led his men in a seemingly impossible attack up the steep, rocky slope, boldly defiant of the annihilating streams of bullets which saturated the area, and despite his own casualty losses and the overwhelming advantage held by the Japanese in superior numbers and dominant position, gained the ridge's top, only to be subjected to an intense barrage of hand grenades thrown by the remaining Japanese staging a suicidal last stand on the reverse slope. When one of the grenades fell in the midst of his surviving men, huddled together in a small trench, Gunnery Sergeant Walsh, in a final valiant act of complete self-sacrifice, instantly threw himself upon the deadly bomb, absorbing with his own body the full and terrific force of the explosion. Through his extraordinary initiative and inspiring valor in the face of almost certain death, he saved his comrades from injury and possible loss of life and enabled his company to seize and hold this vital enemy position. He gallantly gave his life for his country.

Gunnery Sergeant William C. Walsh of Company G, 3/27. *Official USMC Photo*

The blockhouse beside Airfield No. 2 is in Marine hands, but the whole area is being subjected to sheets of Japanese machine-gun fire. Though trapped in the shallow trench, the rifleman is trying to locate a target for himself and the BAR man. *Official USMC Photo*

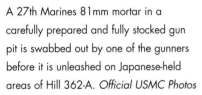

A 27th Marines 81mm mortar in a carefully prepared and fully stocked gun pit is swabbed out by one of the gunners before it is unleashed on Japanese-held areas of Hill 362-A. *Official USMC Photos*

Ammo carriers for a machine-gun squad get ready to rush ahead during the 27th Marines' assault on Hill 362-A, whose tenacious defenders are holding up the left flank of the VAC February 28 advance. *Official USMC Photo*

A company of the 27th Marines climbs a secure section of Hill 362-A's southern slope. *Official USMC Photo*

THE PRESIDENT OF THE UNITED STATES TAKES PRIDE IN PRESENTING
THE MEDAL OF HONOR POSTHUMOUSLY TO

PHARMACIST'S MATE FIRST CLASS JOHN H. WILLIS
UNITED STATES NAVY

FOR SERVICE AS SET FORTH IN THE FOLLOWING CITATION:

For conspicuous gallantry and intrepidity at the risk of his life above and beyond the call of duty as Platoon Corpsman serving with the 3d Battalion, 27th Marines, 5th Marine Division, during operations against enemy Japanese forces on Iwo Jima, Volcano Islands, 28 February 1945. Constantly imperiled by artillery and mortar fire from strong and mutually supporting pillboxes and caves studding Hill 362 in the enemy's cross-island defenses, Willis resolutely administered first aid to the many Marines wounded during the furious close-in fighting until he himself was struck by shrapnel and was ordered back to the battle-aid station. Without waiting for official medical release, he quickly returned to his company and, during a savage hand-to-hand enemy counterattack, daringly advanced to the extreme front lines under mortar and sniper fire to aid a Marine lying wounded in a shellhole. Completely unmindful of his own danger as the Japanese intensified their attack, Willis calmly continued to administer blood plasma to his patient, promptly returning the first hostile grenade which landed in the shellhole while he was working and hurling back seven more in quick succession before the ninth one exploded in his hand and instantly killed him. By his great personal valor in saving others at the sacrifice of his own life, he inspired his companions, although terrifically outnumbered, to launch a fiercely determined attack and repulse the enemy force. His exceptional fortitude and courage in the performance of duty reflect the highest credit upon Willis and the U.S. Naval Service. He gallantly gave his life for his country.

Pharmacist's Mate First Class John H. Willis of 3/27. *Official USN Photo*

This 70mm battalion gun was pulled from a captured dugout on Hill 362-A. Thought diminutive, this weapon was quite lethal. *Official USMC Photo*

A pipe-smoking Marine reconnaissance scout shares cover with a dead and bloating Japanese officer as he looks over the route his unit might have to take into the next day's fight. *Official USMC Photo*

Replacements line up at the Company H, 3/26, command post after the company has been withdrawn from the lines to reequip and rest. The replacements, no doubt drawn from the replacement drafts providing beach labor, do not come close to making good Company H's frightful combat losses. The company is down to no more than 35 effectives on February 28, and if it is lucky it will go back into the fight with about 70, a third of its authorized strength. Key specialists and even company-grade officers and noncommissioned officers bound for command assignments joined combat units from the replacement drafts. *Official USMC Photo*

(continued from page 190)

rolling artillery barrage, all the way to Motoyama village and the high ground commanding Airfield No. 3. To the right, in the 4th Marine Division zone, the 23d Marines was unable to regain its foothold on Hill 382, but the 25th Marines' advance along the east coast was stopped cold in front of Minami. On the VAC left, the 5th Marine Division's 27th Marines, fighting toward Nishi village, drove to the southern slope of Hill 362-A. Also, the 28th Marines, which had finished mopping up the Suribachi area while standing by as the VAC reserve, was alerted to take part in the northern drive. During the

Time out for a quickie. Within the limitations imposed by a Spartan environment, every effort was made to allow Marines rotating from the front to feel human. Things as simple as a shower and a shave could do wonders. *Official USMC Photo*

These 1/26 Marines are taking time out during their brief respite in the rear to remember fallen comrades.
Official USMC Photo

The original caption for this sobering February 28 photo reads: "The Power and the Price — The power of the invasion armada (background) stands out in ironic contrast with the scene on the Iwo Jima beach. Marines of the 3d Division, covered with their ponchos, lie on the beach they gave their lives to win. A few thousand yards away the battle was still on." *Official USMC Photo*

night, Major General Graves Erskine asked that his third regimental combat team, built around the 3d Marines, be detached from the FMFPac reserve and sent ashore to rejoin the 3d Marine Division. VAC endorsed the request, and so did Vice Admiral Kelly Turner, but Holland Smith thought the troops would not be needed, so he refused the request, a decision it was his right to make even though no one else understood why he made it that way.

CHAPTER 15

To Victory

The strategic phase of the Iwo Jima campaign came to an end when Airfield No. 2 fully fell into Marine hands. V Amphibious Corps still had a long way to go, and it would be hard fighting all the way. Marines did not know that the last of the Japanese garrison's water supply had fallen into their hands; there were no discernible signs of it at first. But that milestone was as important as the fall of the airfields, for it limited the near-term ability of the Japanese to mount an effective counterassault operation. Stoic as the Japanese soldier was, the loss of his last reliable water supply no doubt had as brutal an effect on his morale as it did on his physical well-being and combat effectiveness.

The defenders remained stubborn and resolute despite the fact that they were plainly losing. As March began, there was no slackening of the defense; ground north of Airfield No. 2 was as difficult and expensive to take as ground to the south had been. Moreover, the Marines knew that their own combat effectiveness was waning. No fresh units would be committed, and the replacement drafts were dwindling rapidly. All combat units were massively understrength.

D+10

On March 1, the 3d Marine Division had to commit both of its infantry regiments, the 9th and the 21st, at the same time. In the 5th Division zone, the newly committed 28th Marines finished off the defenders on Hill 362-A, but there were almost no other gains, and the 4th Division was ferociously opposed around Hill 382.

It's time to move out again.
Official USMC Photo

A dead Japanese soldier beside a dead Japanese light tank. *Official USMC*

Marine infantrymen maneuver as a Sherman sets fire to a Japanese emplacement or cave. *Official USMC Photo*

During the day, Marine transport planes based in the Marianas air-dropped whole blood, ammunition, spare parts, and mail; and an advance echelon of VMO-1 arrived by ship from Guam. The escort carriers embarking spare airplanes and pilots for the air support flotilla retired toward Ulithi in anticipation of the upcoming Okinawa operation. This was a sign that the Pacific high command now thought of the battle for Iwo as a done deal.

D+11

On March 2, the 3d Marine Division plunged forward in the VAC center and took most of the uncompleted Airfield No. 3, but it then bogged down as it tried to mount a

The 2.36-inch rocket launcher, known as the bazooka, came into its own on Pacific battlefields, where Japanese tanks were few and Japanese emplacements were many. The blast from a bazooka's shaped-charge warhead could penetrate many bunker and pillbox walls or enlarge firing apertures to make them easier to hit by other weapons systems. *Official USMC Photo*

flank attack into the 5th Division zone, where the 28th Marines was encountering stiff opposition before Nishi Ridge. (During the afternoon, Lieutenant Colonel Chandler Johnson, whose idea it had been to raise the national colors over Suribachi, was killed by friendly artillery as he reconnoitered the 2/28 front.) The 4th Division's 24th Marines spent the day clearing Hill 382, while the 25th Marines was fully committed to reducing a reentrant near Minami. All across the VAC front, the opposing forces were too close to one another for effective Marine artillery support, and Marine tanks were often held at bay by the jumbled terrain.

Seabees working on Airfield No. 1 announced that the main runway, now completed to a length of 4,700 feet, was fully operational for transport planes. In short order, a Navy R4D medical transport arrived from the Marianas to evacuate twelve wounded Marines by air. Several Marine transports also were dispatched from Saipan during the day to deliver emergency supplies of 81mm mortar ammunition, which had been in chronically short supply from D+1 onward. All of these transports landed, unloaded, and flew home safely despite intermittent targeting of the airfield by Japanese mortars.

Also on March 2, unloading operations got under way on the newly cleared and leveled western beaches, in the 5th Marine Division rear.

As the air evacuation operation from Iwo to the Marianas ramps up, these wounded 4th Division Marines have been staged beside a hospital plane for loading. They have already been treated and, as necessary, undergone surgery at one of a handful of hospitals near Airfield No. 1. They might undergo additional surgery at one of the Pacific rear bases or be flown all the way to the United States for further hospital care. *Official USMC Photo*

Flight nurses accompanied nearly every evacuation flight from Iwo to the Marianas. *Official USMC Photo*

Air Evacuation

Transports, large and small, were loaded expeditiously with the means at hand, each taking a full load of litter cases and walking wounded—whatever it took to clear the hospitals for the never-ending influx from the front. Wounded men whose injuries could not weather high altitudes continued to be evacuated by ship. *Official USMC Photos*

This photo was taken aboard the first medical evacuation flight to leave Iwo. As a rule, doctors, army medics or navy hospital corpsmen, and nurses accompanied each flight to monitor the patients as well as to take care of unanticipated problems. *Official USMC Photo*

Another planeload of wounded lifts off from Iwo. The tents in the foreground comprise one the hospitals set up next to Airfield No. 1. *Official USMC Photo*

Corporal Charles J. Berry of 1/26.
Official USMC Photo

THE PRESIDENT OF THE UNITED STATES TAKES PRIDE IN PRESENTING
THE MEDAL OF HONOR POSTHUMOUSLY TO

CORPORAL CHARLES J. BERRY
UNITED STATES MARINE CORPS

FOR SERVICE AS SET FORTH IN THE FOLLOWING CITATION:

For conspicuous gallantry and intrepidity at the risk of his life above and beyond the call of duty as member of a machine-gun crew, serving with the 1st Battalion, 26th Marines, 5th Marine Division, in action against enemy Japanese forces during the seizure of Iwo Jima in the Volcano Islands, on 3 March 1945. Stationed in the front lines, Corporal Berry manned his weapon with alert readiness as he maintained a constant vigil with other members of his gun crew during the hazardous night hours. When infiltrating Japanese soldiers launched a surprise attack shortly after midnight in an attempt to overrun his position, he engaged in a pitched hand-grenade duel, returning the dangerous weapons with prompt and deadly accuracy until an enemy grenade landed in the foxhole. Determined to save his comrades, he unhesitatingly chose to sacrifice himself and immediately dived on the deadly missile, absorbing the shattering violence of the exploding charge in his own body and protecting the others from serious injury. Stouthearted and indomitable, Corporal Berry fearlessly yielded his own life that his fellow Marines might carry on the relentless battle against a ruthless enemy, and his superb valor and unfaltering devotion to duty in the face of certain death reflect the highest credit upon himself and upon the United States Naval Service. He gallantly gave his life for his country.

D+12

The March 3 ground attacks achieved uneven results; some units were held to a virtual standstill, while others sprang forward. A combination of attacks managed to isolate the defenders of Minami in a pocket on the 4th Division's right flank. Fighting was especially intense in the 5th Division zone.

A Japanese twin-engine land-based reconnaissance plane was shot down by a pair of escort-based fighters at 1215 hours. As far as anyone could figure, the Iwo garrison was out of touch with Japan and the airplane was sent to see what it could see.

This Japanese prisoner of war, overseen by a 4th Marine Division language officer, is aboard an LCI(G) offshore northern Iwo to broadcast a scripted surrender plea via loudspeaker to former comrades holding out in seaside caves and bunkers. On the whole, using prisoners to talk other Japanese into giving up was a successful venture. *Official USMC Photo*

Marines from 3/23 move toward the front lines to deliver another attack. *Official USMC Photo*

Private First Class William R. Caddy of Company I, 3/26. *Official USMC Photo*

THE PRESIDENT OF THE UNITED STATES TAKES PRIDE IN PRESENTING THE MEDAL OF HONOR POSTHUMOUSLY TO

PRIVATE FIRST CLASS WILLIAM R. CADDY
UNITED STATES MARINE CORS RESERVE

FOR SERVICE AS SET FORTH IN THE FOLLOWING CITATION:

For conspicuous gallantry and intrepidity at the risk of his life above and beyond the call of duty while serving as a rifleman with Company I, 3d Battalion, 26th Marines, 5th Marine Division, in action against enemy Japanese forces during the seizure of Iwo Jima in the Volcano Islands, 3 March 1945. Consistently aggressive, Private First Class Caddy boldly defied shattering Japanese machine-gun and small-arms fire to move forward with his platoon leader and another Marine during a determined advance of his company through an isolated sector and, gaining the comparative safety of a shell hole, took temporary cover with his comrades. Immediately pinned down by deadly sniper fire from a well-concealed position, he made several unsuccessful attempts to again move forward and then, joined by his platoon leader, engaged the enemy in a fierce exchange of hand grenades until a Japanese grenade fell in the shell hole. Fearlessly disregarding all personal danger, Private First Class Caddy instantly threw himself upon the deadly missile, absorbing the exploding charge in his own body and protecting the others from serious injury. Stouthearted and indomitable, he unhesitatingly yielded his own life that his fellow Marines might carry on the relentless battle against a fanatic enemy. His dauntless courage and valiant spirit of self-sacrifice in the face of certain death reflect the highest credit upon Private First Class Caddy and the United States Naval Service. He gallantly gave his life for his country.

The shooter has spotted a Japanese in the open. As the system of interconnecting caves was interdicted by the Marine advance, more and more Japanese had to expose themselves on the surface to carry messages, retreat, or move elsewhere in the remaining defenses. *Official USMC Photo*

Sergeant William G. Harrell of 1/28.
Official USMC Photo

THE PRESIDENT OF THE UNITED STATES TAKES PRIDE IN PRESENTING
THE MEDAL OF HONOR TO

SERGEANT WILLIAM G. HARRELL
UNITED STATES MARINE CORPS

FOR SERVICE AS SET FORTH IN THE FOLLOWING CITATION:

For conspicuous gallantry and intrepidity at the risk of his life above and beyond the call of duty as Leader of an assault group, serving with the 1st Battalion, 28th Marines, 5th Marine Division, during hand-to-hand combat with enemy Japanese at Iwo Jima, Volcano Islands, on 3 March 1945. Standing watch alternately with another Marine in a terrain studded with caves and ravines, Sergeant Harrell was holding a position in a perimeter defense around the company command post when Japanese troops infiltrated our lines in the early hours of dawn. Awakened by a sudden attack, he quickly opened fire with his carbine and killed two of the enemy as they emerged from a ravine in the light of a star-shell burst. Unmindful of his danger as hostile grenades fell closer, he waged a fierce lone battle until an exploding missile tore off his left hand and fractured his thigh; he was attempting to reload the carbine when his companion returned from the command post with another weapon. Wounded again by a Japanese who rushed the foxhole wielding a saber in the darkness, Sergeant Harrell succeeded in drawing his pistol and killing his opponent and then ordered his wounded companion to a place of safety. Exhausted by profuse bleeding but still unbeaten, he fearlessly met the challenge of two more enemy troops who charged his position and placed a grenade near his head. Killing one man with his pistol, he grasped the sputtering grenade with his good right hand and, pushing it painfully toward the crouching soldier, saw his remaining assailant destroyed but his own hand severed in the explosion. At dawn Sergeant Harrell was evacuated from a position hedged by the bodies of twelve dead Japanese, at least five of whom he had personally destroyed in his self-sacrificing defense of the command post. His grim fortitude, exceptional valor and indomitable fighting spirit against almost insurmountable odds reflect the highest credit upon himself and enhance the finest traditions of the United States Naval Service.

THE PRESIDENT OF THE UNITED STATES TAKES PRIDE IN PRESENTING
THE MEDAL OF HONOR TO

PHARMACIST'S MATE SECOND CLASS GEORGE E. WAHLEN
UNITED STATES NAVY

FOR SERVICE AS SET FORTH IN THE FOLLOWING CITATION:

For conspicuous gallantry and intrepidity at the risk of his life above and beyond the call of duty while serving with the 2d Battalion, 26th Marines, 5th Marine Division, during action against enemy Japanese forces on Iwo Jima in the Volcano group on 3 March 1945. Painfully wounded in the bitter action on 26 February, Wahlen remained on the battlefield, advancing well forward of the front lines to aid a wounded Marine and carrying him back to safety despite a terrific concentration of fire. Tireless in his ministrations, he consistently disregarded all danger to attend his fighting comrades as they fell under the devastating rain of shrapnel and bullets, and rendered prompt assistance to various elements of his combat group as required. When an adjacent platoon suffered heavy casualties, he defied the continuous pounding of heavy mortars and deadly fire of enemy rifles to care for the wounded, working rapidly in an area swept by constant fire and treating 14 casualties before returning to his own platoon. Wounded again on 2 March, he gallantly refused evacuation, moving out with his company the following day in a furious assault across 600 yards of open terrain and repeatedly rendering medical aid while exposed to the blasting fury of powerful Japanese guns. Stouthearted and indomitable, he persevered in his determined efforts as his unit waged fierce battle and, unable to walk after sustaining a third agonizing wound, resolutely crawled 50 yards to administer first aid to still another fallen fighter. By his dauntless fortitude and valor, Wahlen served as a constant inspiration and contributed vitally to the high morale of his company during critical phases of this strategically important engagement. His heroic spirit of self-sacrifice in the face of overwhelming enemy fire upheld the highest traditions of the U.S. Naval Service.

Pharmacist's Mate Second Class George E. Wahlen of 2/26. *Official USN Photo*

D+13

On March 4, six Marine regiments attempted to advance abreast, but there were almost no gains anywhere along the VAC line.

During the afternoon, an air controller aboard an air-sea rescue ship offshore Iwo received an emergency message from the radioman aboard the 9th Very Heavy Bombardment Group's B-29 *Dinah Might*, piloted by 1st Lieutenant R. Fred Malo. Airfield No. 1 was not yet accredited to land heavy bombers, but no one was about to turn a needy air crew away from a safe haven purchased at such a high and growing price. Landing directions were given, but

The successful landing of the B-29 *Dinah Might* drew hundreds of gawkers and well-wishers. This B-29 had a defective fuel valve that might have forced it to ditch at sea, possibly with the loss of life. The valve was replaced and *Dinah Might* took off the same day it landed, March 4. *Official USMC Photo*

Pharmacist's Mate 3d Class Jack Williams of 3/28. *Official USN Photo*

THE PRESIDENT OF THE UNITED STATES TAKES PRIDE IN PRESENTING
THE MEDAL OF HONOR POSTHUMOUSLY TO

PHARMACIST'S MATE THIRD CLASS JACK WILLIAMS
UNITED STATES NAVAL RESERVE

FOR SERVICE AS SET FORTH IN THE FOLLOWING CITATION:

For conspicuous gallantry and intrepidity at the risk of his life above and beyond the call of duty while serving with the 3d Battalion, 28th Marines, 5th Marine Division, during the occupation of Iwo Jima Volcano Islands, 3 March 1945. Gallantly going forward on the front lines under intense enemy small-arms fire to assist a Marine wounded in a fierce grenade battle, Williams dragged the man to a shallow depression and was kneeling, using his own body as a screen from the sustained fire as he administered first aid, when struck in the abdomen and groin three times by hostile rifle fire. Momentarily stunned, he quickly recovered and completed his ministration before applying battle dressings to his own multiple wounds. Unmindful of his own urgent need for medical attention, he remained in the perilous fire-swept area to care for another Marine casualty. Heroically completing his task despite pain and profuse bleeding, he then endeavored to make his way to the rear in search of adequate aid for himself when struck down by a Japanese sniper bullet, which caused his collapse. Succumbing later as a result of his self-sacrificing service to others, Williams, by his courageous determination, unwavering fortitude and valiant performance of duty, served as an inspiring example of heroism, in keeping with the highest traditions of the U.S. Naval Service. He gallantly gave his life for his country.

One measure of progress is how quickly an infantry company's 60mm mortars have to advance. This one appears to have come to rest for quite a while. *Official USMC Photo*

Dinah Might's crew noted it was a downwind heading. It took a moment to explain that a standard upwind approach would bring the bomber in over Japanese guns. The bomber came in beside Suribachi and set its wheels down right at the southern end of the runway. It was a good landing and a historic moment: it was the first proof of what Iwo was for, the first of more than two thousand landings by B-29s on the island. (The Malo crew made another such landing, but then all but one of them died over Japan or in a crash at Tinian.)

D+14

March 5 was largely a day off. No new attacks were ordered as all three divisions reorganized their front-line units in anticipation of a renewed offensive. For the first time, the 5th Marine Division moved all three of its regimental combat teams to the front line, leaving just one VAC regiment, the 23d Marines, as a reserve. Indeed, FMFPac thought matters were so much in hand that the 3d Marine Division's reinforced 3d Marines was released from the expeditionary reserve and ordered out of the area.

For all that it was a day off, Marine units sustained approximately four hundred casualties at the hands of Japanese guns, mortars, and rockets.

D+15

March 6 opened with the heaviest and most concentrated artillery and naval gunfire preparation of the campaign. VAC jumped off on schedule against opposition so heavy and so bitter that gains were reported as negligible. The longest advance of the day was registered in the center, by the 21st Marines, which drove forward a disappointing 200 yards. Nevertheless, the 25th Marines mopped up the Minami pocket.

The VII Fighter Command's commanding general landed on Airfield No. 1 in the lead of 28 P-51 long-range fighters and a dozen P-61 twin-engine night fighters, the first American aircraft to be permanently based on Iwo. Ground personnel to service the aircraft were flown in from Guam aboard Marine and Army Air Forces transport planes that evacuated Marine wounded on the return flight. Later in the day, several navy PB4Y land-based patrol bombers arrived for permanent duty as replacements for the amphibian PBMs, which had been experiencing no end of difficulties due to heavy seas.

Marine riflemen prepare to assault a Japanese-held cave, but first the bazookaman higher up will try to weaken it. *Official USMC Photo*

THE BUREAUCRACY
OF DEATH

Official USMC Photo

Official USMC Photo

Marine infantrymen pause behind cover before advancing across a wide stretch of flat, open ground. Ahead, several Shermans are taking on Japanese emplacements without the usual close infantry cover. *Official USMC Photo*

D+16

The March 7 assault was launched without preparatory fires, which did little to lull the defenders into a false sense of security. Results were wildly uneven, with small gains throughout the 3d Marine Division zone, in the VAC center, and in the 4th Marine Division zone, on the VAC right, but there was a 600-yard penetration along the west coast by 5th Marine Division troops. On the support front, the margin for error within the shrinking Japanese holdings had become so problematic for naval gunfire that most of the Fifth Fleet's gunfire force was ordered to stand down and retire to Ulithi to prepare for the invasion of Okinawa.

The navy fighters and light bombers aboard Task Group 52.2 escort carriers flew their last ground-support missions of the campaign, and the antisubmarine escort carrier USS *Anzio* retired toward Ulithi. That evening, the P-61 night fighters that had arrived on March 6 flew their first patrol missions centered on Iwo.

Finally, on March 7, the island commander-designate, an Army Air Forces general, assumed responsibility for base development, thus pointing up the fact that Iwo's strategic imperative had officially changed over to support of the B-29 bombing offensive.

P-51s of the VII Fighter Command are armed with 500-pound bombs as preparations are made for their first ground-support mission over Iwo. *Official Signal Corps Photo*

THE PRESIDENT OF THE UNITED STATES TAKES PRIDE IN PRESENTING THE MEDAL OF HONOR TO

SECOND LIEUTENANT JOHN H. LEIMS
UNITED STATES MARINE CORPS RESERVE

FOR SERVICE AS SET FORTH IN THE FOLLOWING CITATION:

For conspicuous gallantry and intrepidity at the risk of his life above and beyond the call of duty as Commanding Officer of Company B, 1st Battalion, 9th Marines, 3d Marine Division, in action against enemy Japanese forces on Iwo Jima in the Volcano Islands, on 7 March 1945. Launching a surprise attack against the rock-embedded fortifications of a dominating Japanese hill position, Second Lieutenant Leims spurred his company forward with indomitable determination and, skillfully directing his assault platoons against the cave-emplaced enemy troops and heavily fortified pillboxes, succeeded in capturing the objective in the late afternoon. When it became apparent that his assault platoons were cut off in this newly won position, approximately four hundred yards forward of adjacent units and lacking all communication with the command post, he personally advanced and laid telephone lines across the isolating expanse of open, fire-swept terrain. Ordered to withdraw his command after he had joined his forward platoons, he immediately complied, adroitly effecting the withdrawal of his troops without incident. Upon arriving at the rear, he was informed that several casualties had been left at the abandoned ridge position beyond the front lines. Although suffering acutely from strain and exhaustion of battle, he instantly went forward despite darkness and the slashing fury of hostile machine-gun fire, located and carried to safety one seriously wounded Marine and then, running the gauntlet of enemy fire for the third time that night, again made his tortuous way into the bullet-riddled deathtrap and rescued another of his wounded men. A dauntless leader, concerned at all times for the welfare of his men, Second Lieutenant Leims soundly maintained the coordinated strength of his battle-wearied company under extremely difficult conditions and, by his bold tactics, sustained aggressiveness and heroic disregard of all personal danger, contributed essentially to the success of his division's operations against this vital Japanese base. His valiant conduct in the face of fanatic opposition sustained and enhanced the highest traditions of the United States Marine Corps.

Second Lieutenant John H. Leims of Company B, 1/9. *Official USMC Photo*

A Joint Assault Signal Company (JASCO) team camps out on high ground in the 4th Marine Division zone to spot targets for air, artillery, and naval gunfire. *Official USMC Photo*

D+17

On March 8, attacking behind artillery and the remnant of naval gunfire support, V Amphibious Corps once again turned in an uneven showing. The 9th Marines, in the corps center, lunged ahead 400 yards, and the adjacent 21st Marines reached the O-3 line. On the right, the 23d Marines made small but steady gains until stopped in its tracks by a forceful counterattack.

Guided by a navy TBM, Army Air Forces P-51s equipped with bombs and machine guns flew their maiden ground-support mission over northern Iwo. During the day, as an advance detachment of a Marine TBM squadron arrived ashore, nearly all the escort carriers remaining at Iwo retired to Ulithi. During their service at Iwo, beginning on February 15, the specially trained and specially equipped ground-support airmen completed more than eight thousand sorties at the cost of 83 aircraft, including operational losses and aboard the USS *Bismarck Sea* when she was sunk by kamikazes.

Private First Class James D. LaBelle of Weapons Company, 27th Marines.
Official USMC Photo

THE PRESIDENT OF THE UNITED STATES TAKES PRIDE IN PRESENTING THE MEDAL OF HONOR POSTHUMOUSLY TO

PRIVATE FIRST CLASS JAMES D. LABELLE
UNITED STATES MARINE CORPS RESERVE

FOR SERVICE AS SET FORTH IN THE FOLLOWING CITATION:

For conspicuous gallantry and intrepidity at the risk of his life above and beyond the call of duty while serving with the Weapons Company, 27th Marines, 5th Marine Division, in action against enemy Japanese forces during the seizure of Iwo Jima in the Volcano Islands, 8 March 1945. Filling a gap in the front lines during a critical phase of the battle, Private First Class LaBelle had dug into a foxhole with two other Marines, and grimly aware of the enemy's persistent attempts to blast a way through our lines with hand grenades, applied himself with steady concentration to maintaining a sharply vigilant watch during the hazardous night hours. Suddenly a hostile grenade landed beyond reach in his foxhole. Quickly estimating the situation, he determined to save the others if possible, shouted a warning, and instantly dived on the missile, absorbing the exploding charge in his own body and thereby protecting his comrades from serious injury. Stouthearted and indomitable, he had unhesitatingly relinquished his own chance of survival that his fellow Marines might carry on the relentless fight against a fanatic enemy, and his dauntless courage, cool decision and valiant spirit of self-sacrifice in the face of certain death reflect the highest credit upon Private First Class LaBelle and the United States Naval Service. He gallantly gave his life in the service of his country.

The President of the United States takes pride in presenting the Medal of Honor posthumously to

First Lieutenant Jack Lummus
United States Marine Corps Reserve

for service as set forth in the following citation:

For conspicuous gallantry and intrepidity at the risk of his life above and beyond the call of duty as leader of a rifle platoon, attached to Company E, 2d Battalion, 27th Marines, 5th Marine Division, in action against enemy Japanese forces on Iwo Jima in the Volcano Islands, 8 March 1945. Resuming his assault tactics with bold decision after fighting without respite for two days and nights, First Lieutenant Lummus slowly advanced his platoon against an enemy deeply entrenched in a network of mutually supporting positions. Suddenly halted by a terrific concentration of hostile fire, he unhesitatingly moved forward of his front line in an effort to neutralize the Japanese position. Although knocked to the ground when an enemy grenade exploded close by, he immediately recovered himself and, again moving forward despite the intensified barrage, quickly located, attacked and destroyed the occupied emplacement. Instantly taken under fire by the garrison of a supporting pillbox and further assailed by the slashing fury of hostile rifle fire, he fell under the impact of a second enemy grenade, but courageously disregarding painful shoulder wounds, staunchly continued his heroic one-man assault and charged the second pillbox, annihilating all the occupants. Subsequently returning to his platoon position, he fearlessly traversed his lines under fire, encouraging his men to advance and directing the fire of supporting tanks against other stubbornly holding Japanese emplacements. Held up again by a devastating barrage, he again moved into the open, rushed a third heavily fortified installation and killed the defending enemy. Determined to crush all resistance, he led his men indomitably, personally attacking foxholes and spider traps with his carbine and systematically reducing the fanatic opposition until, stepping on a land mine, he sustained fatal wounds. By his outstanding valor, skilled tactics and tenacious perseverance in the face of overwhelming odds, First Lieutenant Lummus had inspired his stouthearted Marines to continue the relentless drive northward, thereby contributing materially to the success of his company's mission. His dauntless leadership and unwavering devotion to duty throughout enhanced and sustained the highest traditions of the United States Naval Service. He gallantly gave his life in the service of his country.

First Lieutenant Jack Lummus of Company E, 2/27. *Official USMC Photo*

Platoon Sergeant Joseph R. Julian of
1/27. *Official USMC Photo*

D+18

The big news on March 9 was the breakthrough by the 3d Marine Division to the northern coast. This permanently bifurcated the defending force. Once on its objective, the 3d Division dispatched combat units to mop up bypassed pockets and fighting positions in its zone. The 5th Division made some progress along the west coast, but little was gained elsewhere in its zone or by the 4th Division. Now that the situation ashore was so

A 23d Marines patrol scouts Tachiiwa Point in northeastern Iwo. *Official USMC Photo*

As long as they were able, the Japanese fired guns, mortars, and rockets deep into the VAC rear to shake up, maim, or kill whomever they could and to slow things down as much as possible. Here, flight operations are on hold while a VAC bomb-disposal team digs out a large rocket that failed to detonate. In the distance is a VII Fighter Command P-61 night fighter. *Official USMC Photo*

obviously well in hand, Vice Admiral Kelly Turner decided it was time to sail for Guam, where he could begin to take part in the planning for the invasion of Japan.

Army Air Forces P-51s and P-61s, navy PB4Ys, and Marine TBMs operating from Airfield No. 1 assumed full responsibility for air operations over and around Iwo. A second detachment of Marine TBMs arrived during the day.

D+19

And so it went. The weakened and weakening Marine divisions went up against the weaker and more rapidly weakening Japanese defenders, slowly dismantling the interlocking defensive zones and firing batteries, killing more Japanese than they were losing Americans, and generally driving the living defenders into less tenable but more concentrated defenses.

On March 10 the 4th Marine Division noted that the defense in its zone was perceptibly weaker, and on that day the 23d Marines pushed patrols through to the east coast and on to Tachiiwa Point. On the other hand, the 5th Marine Division was held to minimal gains in nearly impenetrable terrain.

D+20

On March 11, the 4th Division reported the end of organized resistance on the VAC right front, except in one small pocket on the far right. The 5th Division once again made negligible gains in frightful terrain, and the 3d Division continued to mop up in its zone.

The very last detachment of U.S. Navy escort carriers retired to Ulithi.

In the first view, a BAR man (right) and a carbine-armed rifleman search for the Japanese who set the Sherman's engine on fire. In the second view, the BAR man locates a suspect and opens fire.
Official USMC Photos

D+21

By March 12, only the 5th Division had a real fight on its hands. All the available air, artillery, and naval gunfire that could safely bear was fired into the division's shrinking objective area, but gains were once again spotty, although the defenders seemed to be putting less heart into their work—no doubt a combination of hunger, thirst, plummeting morale, and having their brains so vigorously rattled. More and more shell-shocked defenders were falling passively into Marine hands, and more and more Japanese were willfully surrendering.

Official USMC Photo

Intense mortar and machine-gun fire have forced these stretcher bearers and the infantrymen nearby to take cover behind a tiny knoll. *Official USMC Photo*

The three airfields on Iwo were renamed South, Center, and North and South Field's by-now 5,800-foot runway was declared operational even though it had been in constant operation since March 3.

D+21

On March 13, air support was all but obviated due to the extremely small zone remaining to the Japanese and the extremely close fighting quarters the Marines were maintaining. Indeed, all requests by VAC units for air support were denied by Marine and Army air commanders on grounds of safety because the battlefield had become so restricted. There were still plenty of defended caves in the 5th Marine Division zone, but fewer and fewer pillboxes and bunkers were encountered.

D+22

V Amphibious Corps held an official flag-raising ceremony on the morning of March 14, and the first units of the 4th Marine Division were reembarked. The 27th Marines gained 600 yards on the 5th Marine Division right flank as VII Fighter Command P-51s mounted the final air support mission of the campaign. Army Air Forces warplanes based on Iwo and in the Marianas would mount numerous missions against bypassed islands in the area, but air operations against targets on Iwo had ended.

As the front lines advance, Marine engineers and Seabees extend and improve the road net throughout the rear. *Official USMC Photo*

This assault team has moved on a pillbox from its blind side, and the flamethower is firing burning fuel directly into the firing aperture. Note the plumes of smoke rising from other, perhaps interconnected, spots nearby. *Official USMC Photo*

Two Japanese emerge from the smoke-shrouded entrance of a hillside cave. *Official USMC Photo*

After emptying one magazine into the cave, a wary BAR man, with finger on the trigger of his reloaded weapon, gives instructions to his back-up as he stands over the narrow entrance. No doubt this cave entrance was impossible to see until the attackers were right on top of it. *Official USMC Photo*

VAC's *official* flag-raising at Iwo Jima on March 14 was held with great panoply—speeches and bugle calls—but it didn't come close in emotive power to both of the unofficial flag ceremonies atop Suribachi on February 23.
Official USMC Photo

Private George Phillips of 2/28.
Official USMC Photo

THE PRESIDENT OF THE UNITED STATES TAKES PRIDE IN PRESENTING THE MEDAL OF HONOR POSTHUMOUSLY TO

PRIVATE GEORGE PHILLIPS
UNITED STATES MARINE CORPS RESERVE

FOR SERVICE AS SET FORTH IN THE FOLLOWING CITATION:

For conspicuous gallantry and intrepidity at the risk of his life above and beyond the call of duty while serving with the 2d Battalion, 28th Marines, 5th Marine Division, in action against enemy Japanese forces during the seizure of Iwo Jima in the Volcano Islands on 14 March 1945. Standing the foxhole watch while other members of his squad rested after a night of bitter hand-grenade fighting against infiltrating Japanese troops, Private Phillips was the only member of his unit alerted when an enemy hand grenade was tossed into their midst. Instantly shouting a warning, he unhesitatingly threw himself on the deadly missile, absorbing the shattering violence of the exploding charge in his own body and protecting his comrades from serious injury. Stouthearted and indomitable, Private Phillips willingly yielded his own life that his fellow Marines might carry on the relentless battle against a fanatic enemy and his superb valor and unfaltering spirit of self-sacrifice in the face of certain death reflect the highest credit upon himself and upon the United States Naval Service. He gallantly gave his life for his country.

During a brief lull, a 4th Marine Division infantry company commander discusses options with his men for taking down a large blockhouse that is holding up the company's advance.
Official USMC Photo

THE PRESIDENT OF THE UNITED STATES TAKES PRIDE IN PRESENTING THE MEDAL OF HONOR TO

PRIVATE FRANKLIN E. SIGLER
UNITED STATES MARINE CORPS RESERVE

FOR SERVICE AS SET FORTH IN THE FOLLOWING CITATION:

For conspicuous gallantry and intrepidity at the risk of his life above and beyond the call of duty while serving with the 2d Battalion, 26th Marines, 5th Marine Division, in action against enemy Japanese forces during the seizure of Iwo Jima in the Volcano Islands on 14 March 1945. Voluntarily taking command of his rifle squad when the leader became a casualty, Private Sigler fearlessly led a bold charge against an enemy gun installation that had held up the advance of his company for several days and, reaching the position in advance of the others, assailed the emplacement with hand grenades and personally annihilated the entire crew. As additional Japanese troops opened fire from concealed tunnels and caves above, he quickly scaled the rocks leading to the attacking guns, surprised the enemy with a furious one-man assault and, although severely wounded in the encounter, deliberately crawled back to his squad position, where he steadfastly refused evacuation, persistently directing heavy machine-gun and rocket barrages on the Japanese cave entrances. Undaunted by the merciless rain of hostile fire during the intensified action, he gallantly disregarded his own painful wounds to aid casualties, carrying three wounded squad members to safety behind the lines and returning to continue the battle with renewed determination until ordered to retire for medical treatment. Stouthearted and indomitable in the face of extreme peril, Private Sigler, by his alert initiative, unfaltering leadership and daring tactics in a critical situation, effected the release of his besieged company from enemy fire and contributed essentially to its further advance against a savagely fighting enemy. His superb valor, resolute fortitude and heroic spirit of self-sacrifice throughout reflect the highest credit upon Private Sigler and the United States Naval Service.

Private Franklin E. Sigler of 2/26.
Official USMC Photo

D+23

As 3d and 4th Marine division troops continued to mop up in the central and eastern sectors, respectively, on March 15, the remaining defenses in the 5th Marine Division zone continued to fall before the heaviest ground assaults the division still could deliver. The last naval gunfire mission of the campaign was fired, but warships remained on station to provide illumination.

THE PRESIDENT OF THE UNITED STATES TAKES PRIDE IN PRESENTING THE MEDAL OF HONOR TO

PHARMACIST'S MATE FIRST CLASS FRANCIS J. PIERCE
UNITED STATES NAVY

FOR SERVICE AS SET FORTH IN THE FOLLOWING CITATION:

For conspicuous gallantry and intrepidity at the risk of his life above and beyond the call of duty while attached to the 2nd Battalion, 24th Marines, 4th Marine Division, during the Iwo Jima campaign on 15 and 16 March 1945. Almost continuously under fire while carrying out the most dangerous volunteer assignment, Petty Officer Pierce gained valuable knowledge of the terrain and disposition of troops. Caught in heavy enemy rifle and machine-gun fire that wounded a corpsman and two of the eight stretcher bearers who were carrying two wounded Marines to a forward aid station on 15 March, Petty Officer Pierce quickly took charge of the party, carried the newly wounded men to a sheltered position, and rendered first aid. After directing the evacuation of three of the casualties, he stood in the open to draw the enemy's fire and, with his weapon blasting, enabled the litter bearers to reach cover. Turning his attention to the other two casualties, he was attempting to stop the profuse bleeding of one man when a Japanese fired from a cave less than 20 yards away and wounded his patient again. Risking his own life to save his patient, Petty Officer Pierce deliberately exposed himself to draw the attacker from the cave and destroyed him with the last of his ammunition. Then lifting the wounded man to his back, he advanced unarmed through deadly rifle fire across 200 feet of open terrain. Despite exhaustion and in the face of warnings against such a suicidal mission, he again traversed the same fire-swept path to rescue the remaining Marine. On the following morning, he led a combat patrol to the snipers' nest and, while aiding a stricken Marine, was seriously wounded. Refusing aid for himself, he directed treatment for the casualty, at the same time maintaining protective fire for his comrades. Completely fearless, and devoted to the care of his patients, Petty Officer Pierce inspired the entire battalion. His valor in the face of extreme peril sustains the finest traditions of the United States Naval Service.

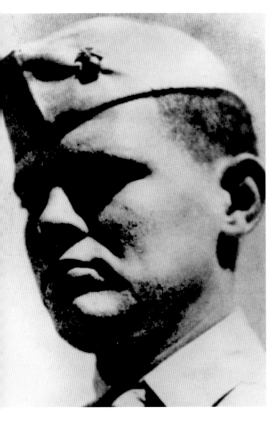

Pharmacist's Mate First Class Francis J. Pierce of 2/24. *Official USN Photo*

Despite heavy fire from their front, 3/28 Marines break cover to advance over the crest of a small rise. *Official USMC Photo*

This Japanese soldier was shot dead in the 3d Marine Division zone. *Official USMC Photo*

D+24

Iwo Jima was declared secure at 1800 on March 16, but organized Japanese units in the far north still offered intense resistance. The 21st Marines attacked westward into the 5th Marine Division zone behind intense artillery fire and drove all the way to Kitano Point, but 5th Marine Division units made only small gains in their shrinking zone. The 27th Marines retired from the battlefield to serve as the VAC reserve, and the 23d Marines was reembarked.

Center Field, which featured a 5,200-foot runway and a 4,800-foot runway, was declared fully operational for use as a staging base for Marianas-based B-29s on their way to and from Japan. By this time, landings—and sometimes crash-landings—by battle-damaged or malfunctioning B-29s had become commonplace, and resupply and medical evacuation flights had long since become routine.

Machine gun carts are pressed into evacuation service by one infantry battalion when a shortage of litters develops. *Official USMC Photo*

This single view should give a good idea of what Marines were up against in northern Iwo. There is a big cave entrance in the center, one directly above it, a firing embrasure at right center and another at the right edge. There might be others on the left side of the photo as well. No doubt they are all integrated within a system that goes far beyond what is seen here.
Official USMC Photo

The original caption for this photo reads: "Flamethrower at work." *Official USMC Photo*

D+25

On March 17, the 5th Marine Division managed to pocket the last organized defenders still under General Kuribayashi's control within a ravine running some 700 yards east to west and 200 to 500 yards from north to south. This area was too small for the provision of Marine artillery support.

After it completed mopping-up operations in its zone, the 25th Marines was reembarked.

Official USMC Photo

This prisoner appears on the verge of tears as he tells a Marine language officer that he has been holed up in a cave, alone and without food, for ten days. *Official USMC Photo*

This Marine is directing fire for a machine gun whose gunner is unable to see the target. *Official USMC Photo*

A Marine squad halts briefly on a trail just below the summit of a small rise while, to the left, a grenade is hurled at a Japanese emplacement covering the trail. *Official USMC Photo*

It's mighty tight in this rocky ravine as a blade tank inches forward past Marine infantrymen who wait in cover for it to neutralize a Japanese emplacement ahead. *Official USMC Photo*

These Marine riflemen are scrambling up a rock-strewn, lightly wooded slope in an attempt to outflank a Japanese position that is holding up the advance in this area. *Official USMC Photo*

D+26

By March 18, the last American ground units engaged with an organized Japanese force were the 5th Marine Division's 26th and 28th Marines, which pressed slowly in on the final defensive zone. As they did, 5th Division units no longer required on the island were reembarked, and 3d Marine Division units worked throughout the island to take down bypassed positions that remained unsealed.

D+27

The last 4th Marine Division units left Iwo on March 19.

D+28

On March 20, elements of the 26th Marines were withdrawn from the shrinking northern pocket to be reembarked, and the army's independent 147th Infantry Regiment landed to assume some of the mopping-up effort from 3d Marine Division units.

(continued on page 234)

Marines who moments earlier were intent on taking out a Japanese-held cave scramble for cover as a Japanese hand grenade bursts in this rocky ravine. The assault was relaunched before the smoke cleared. *Official USMC Photo*

Leaning on his weapon to gain traction on the uneven ground, a BAR man makes his move toward a stubbornly defended Japanese emplacement. *Official USMC Photo*

Every Marine a rifleman. This is a fabulous study of a Marine rifleman confidently plying his trade. Note that the shooter is perched on a pile of Japanese ammunition boxes. *Official USMC Photo*

Even though he is well covered by half a dozen riflemen, this flamethrower assaultman *really* has no more protection than his helmet, shirt and unfathomable courage. Minutes earlier, the Japanese in this cave refused an opportunity to surrender by tossing a grenade through the entrance. Now there is no more time to waste trying to get them out alive. *Official USMC Photo*

Fire in the hole. This Marine has tossed a grenade into this cave, and now he is asking nicely for the occupants to surrender. *Official USMC Photo*

This 81mm mortar squad is waiting for a call to provide support to the infantry. From D-day onward, the hardworking 81s were plagued by ammunition shortages, a testament to their usefulness. *Official USMC Photo*

CREW-SERVED WEAPONS

The 37mm antitank guns deployed by the regimental weapons companies were reasonably easy to maneuver to the front lines, and their armor-piercing rounds could pierce many emplacements. Extremely accurate at close range, the 37s could often fire rounds through firing apertures and other access points of otherwise formidable bunkers and pillboxes. They also could hammer repeatedly on one spot in a solid wall to create a breach. *Official USMC Photo*

By this late phase of the war, Marine artillery regiments fielded only one 75mm howitzer battalion apiece, and three 105mm battalions, the opposite of its 1942 complement. The Marines retained the 75mm battalions by choice—they could have drawn more 105s—because they felt the smaller, relatively portable pack howitzers matched the expeditionary nature of the Marine Corps. This 75 was probably broken down into its components and reassembled on the front lines to deliver direct fire on a stubborn defensive position that is holding up the infantry advance. *Official USMC Photo*

The regimental weapons companies also fielded M3 tank destroyers—halftracks mounting 75mm guns—but they were few in number and extremely vulnerable to all manner of Japanese fire. The M3 halftracks seen here have just overrun a Japanese 5-inch gun (far left), and the one on the right has just set off explosives or combustibles in a Japanese emplacement. *Official USMC Photo*

Although the Sherman tanks deployed by the divisional tank battalions were vulnerable to no end of mishaps—a flame tank in the first view has fallen through the roof of a Japanese cave or bunker—their status as mobile armored pillboxes made them a favorite of front-line infantrymen all across cave-riddled Iwo. The Sherman in the second view has just fired pointblank into a Japanese emplacement. *Official USMC Photos*

Although at times difficult to manhandle to the front lines with enough ammunition to matter, the .30-caliber water-cooled medium machine gun was much beloved by the troops because of its sheer hitting power. Designed as a defensive weapon and deployed as such during most of the Pacific War, the .30-caliber medium was pushed into a more aggressive front-line role when six were issued to each infantry company in a 1944 reorganization of the standard Marine infantry battalion. It was an excellent weapon for suppressing enemy fire in support of a Marine ground attack from a fixed line, but it could not advance right with the troops because of its weight and bulk. *Official USMC Photo*

Far more portable but somewhat less lethal, the .30-caliber light machine guns issued to every infantry company could easily advance with troops in the assault, a role they held from the very beginning of the war.
Official USMC Photo

A lone Marine is dwarfed by the tortured rock formations in this area of northern Iwo. Smoke from a burning underground sulfur deposit serves as a potentially dangerous backdrop in the event any Japanese are looking on. *Official USMC Photo*

First Lieutenant Harry L. Martin of Company C, 5th Pioneer Battalion *Official USMC Photo*

(continued from page 228)

The End

The 27th Marines reembarked on March 22, and the last units of the 26th Marines were withdrawn from the fight on March 24.

On the morning of March 25, the 28th Marines completed the final reduction of the last pocket of resistance. There was plenty of mopping up left to do. At least several hundred Japanese troops remained in organized units and in good order, but the higher-ranking commanders were all dead—killed in combat or by suicide.

THE PRESIDENT OF THE UNITED STATES TAKES PRIDE IN PRESENTING THE MEDAL OF HONOR POSTHUMOUSLY TO

FIRST LIEUTENANT HARRY L. MARTIN
UNITED STATES MARINE CORPS RESERVE

FOR SERVICE AS SET FORTH IN THE FOLLOWING CITATION:

For conspicuous gallantry and intrepidity at the risk of his life above and beyond the call of duty as platoon leader attached to Company C, 5th Pioneer Battalion, 5th Marine Division, in action against enemy Japanese forces on Iwo Jima, Volcano Islands, 26 March 1945. With his sector of the 5th Pioneer Battalion bivouac area penetrated by a concentrated enemy attack launched a few minutes before dawn, First Lieutenant Martin instantly organized a firing line with the Marines nearest his foxhole and succeeded in checking momentarily the headlong rush of the Japanese. Determined to rescue several of his men trapped in positions overrun by the enemy, he defied intense hostile fire to work his way through the Japanese to the surrounded Marines. Although sustaining two severe wounds, he blasted the Japanese who attempted to intercept him, located his beleaguered men and directed them to their own lines. When four of the infiltrating enemy took possession of an abandoned machine-gun pit and subjected his sector to a barrage of hand grenades, First Lieutenant Martin alone and armed only with a pistol, boldly charged the hostile position and killed all its occupants. Realizing that his remaining comrades could not repulse another organized attack, he called to his men to follow and then charged into the midst of the strong enemy force, firing his weapon and scattering them until he fell, mortally wounded by a grenade. By his outstanding valor, indomitable fighting spirit and tenacious determination in the face of overwhelming odds, First Lieutenant Martin permanently disrupted a coordinated Japanese attack and prevented a greater loss of life in his own and adjacent platoons, and his inspiring leadership and unswerving devotion to duty reflect the highest credit upon himself and the United States Naval Service. He gallantly gave his life in the service of his country.

Two of more than a hundred Japanese killed in bitter hand-to-hand combat inside the 21st Fighter Group encampment. *National Archives and Records*

At about 2100 hours, VII Fighter Command P-61s shot down two (and possibly three) Imperial Navy land-based bombers off Iwo. This was the last known attempt by the Japanese to try to contact or support the survivors in this manner.

On March 26, 111 VII Fighter Command P-51s arrived at Iwo from Hawaii. As soon as their pilots and ground crews could settle in, they would begin to escort B-29s over Japan, thus fulfilling yet another of the Iwo Jima campaign's strategic imperatives.

The defenders' last gasp of any significance was a suicidal attack on the night of March 26–27 by several hundred Japanese upon the bivouac of the VII Fighter Command's newly arrived 21st Fighter Group. Forty-four Army Air Forces personnel, including several pilots, were killed and 88 were wounded in what amounted to a hand-to-hand defense. Marine support units bivouacked near North Field also were engaged. Nearly all the Japanese were killed and the rest were driven off. In the morning, 21st Fighter Group P-51 pilots got in some retribution when they mounted ground attacks against the bypassed garrison on Haha Jima.

After the last banzai attack, the Japanese were methodically hunted down by garrison troops and sealed in their emplacements, caves, and tunnels—or they killed themselves, or died of thirst, starvation, or broken hearts.

The Price

This is a breakdown of American casualties sustained in the battle for Iwo: *Killed*—6,821, of whom 5,931 were Marines, 197 were navy medical personnel, 633 were navy nonmedical personnel and airmen, 51 were Seabees, and 9 were soldiers; *Wounded*—19,217, of whom 17,272 were Marines, 541 were navy medical personnel, 1,158 were navy nonmedical personnel and airmen, 218 were Seabees, and 28 were soldiers; and *Combat Fatigue*—2,647. The grand total is 28,685 American casualties from invasion and garrison units.

On the Japanese side, 1,083 were captured and an estimated 20,000 to 22,000 were killed.

This Marine has suffered an agonizing stomach wound. *Official USMC Photo*

Working in billowing sulfur smoke, a Marine fire team prepares to assault a cave after softening it up with hand grenades. *Official USMC Photo*

FAREWELL

Official USMC Photos

Official USMC Photos

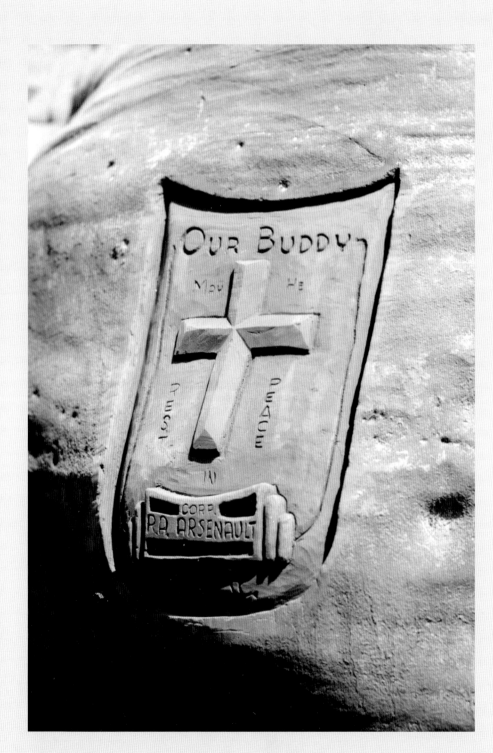

Official USMC Photos

Making use of cover in a shell-shattered 5-inch gun emplacement, two sharp-eyed scouts peer through sulfur smoke in the hope of locating a Japanese emplacement up ahead. *Official USMC Photo*

These troops are waiting for word to commence the assault, straight up the road behind the tank. *Official USMC Photo*

Until the final shot was fired, the stream of casualties never abated. *Official USMC Photo*

The last patrol. These Marines have been sent forward to check the area from which the last shots opposing the VAC offensive were fired. *Official USMC Photo*

Survivors pose with a trophy. The real trophy is the breath in their lungs. *Official USMC Photo*

CHAPTER 16

Justifying Iwo

There is no calculation more brutal than the one that is made to justify an exigency of war. The deaths of one group of people are rationalized to justify the lives of another group of people who get to go on living.

By any stretch of the imagination, the cruel calculus of Iwo Jima is too close to call.

On the American side, 6,821 men died and 19,217 were wounded. These deaths are argued away because the 11-man crews of nearly 2,400 B-29s landed at Iwo for every sort of problem, from bad spark plugs to massive battle damage to just one critically wounded crewman who would not have survived the flight all the way back to Saipan, Tinian, or Guam.

That's the dilemma. More than 26,000 B-29 crewmen landed at Iwo under the rubric of declared emergencies, some more than once. That is nearly four times the number of American servicemen who died to take the island so the airmen could land there. But it is impossible to calculate how many of them owed their lives to a safe landing at Iwo rather than ditching at sea in the hope of being picked up by a string of lifeguard submarines or air-sea rescue planes out of the Marianas. How many malfunctioning B-29s that landed at Iwo—just because it was there—would otherwise have continued on to safe landings in the Marianas—if there had been no other choice?

Looking at it from the other direction clears up nothing. P-51s of the VII Fighter Command that rendezvoused with the B-29s over Japan accounted for scores and scores of Japanese high-altitude home-defense fighters that might otherwise have shot down unknowable numbers of B-29s that, in the end, never landed at Iwo anyway. Or, to add another layer of complexity, how many of those downed Japanese fighters might have

Iwo played a vital role as the base from which VII Fighter Command P-51s sallied to escort B-29s at very high altitudes over central and southern Japan. Note that each Mustang is equipped with two large auxiliary wing tanks.
Official Signal Corps Photo

The Iwo Jima air base complex accommodated the smallest and largest warplanes in the American Pacific War arsenal. Seen here is a Marine OY and a B-29. *Official USMC Photo*

This Navy Consolidated PB4Y-2 Privateer patrol bomber is essentially the same airplane as the Army Air Forces B-24, but it has just one tail fin and rudder. The Privateers operating from Iwo were on the lookout for Japanese warships and submarines, but they certainly did their share to locate downed airmen. *Official USN Photo*

This is the VII Fighter Command air defense control center. If Japanese warplanes had attacked Iwo they would have been met by VII Fighter Command P-51s and P-47s as well as Marine F4U Corsairs, or at night by army P-61 and Marine F6F-5N night fighters. The main role of the P-47s and F4Us was hammering bypassed Japanese garrisons, a job the heavily armed P-61s also undertook, as did Marine TBMs. Iwo also was home to VMB-612, whose radar-guided night-raiding PBJs routinely attacked shipping and harbors in southern Japan. *Official Signal Corps Photo*

Shrouded in dust on South Field by a taxiing Marine TBM is an Army Air Forces Consolidated OA-10 search-and-rescue amphibian bomber—the same airplane as the navy's famous PBY Catalina patrol bomber. Ditched airmen also were picked up by picket ships and lifeguard submarines strung out along flight routes between the Marianas and Japan. *Official USMC Photo*

Relatively few of the nearly 2,400 B-29s reported to have set down at Iwo suffered landing mishaps, but this series of photos provides some insight into how close even getting to Iwo was cutting it for a fair percentage of battle-damaged and malfunctioning very heavy bombers. The first B-29 in the series was towed 130 yards to the beach by landing craft, then hauled ashore and rehabilitated. *Official Signal Corps Photo*

National Archives & Records Administration

Official Signal Corps Photo

Official Signal Corps Photo

Official Signal Corps Photo

damaged B-29s they in fact did not damage, thus necessitating emergency landings at Iwo that never took place?

The Army Air Forces based an air-sea rescue squadron equipped with amphibian aircraft at Iwo, especially to pluck B-29 crews from the sea in the event their damaged or malfunctioning bombers ditched or crash-landed before they could get to Iwo. How many crewmen from these planes would have died at sea if the amphibians had not been based at Iwo?

Of the B-29s themselves that went on to fight another day only because they landed at Iwo, would the permanent loss of large numbers of them have put off the ultimate victory or, at least, permitted Japan to build more fighters to knock down more B-29 crews who were never knocked down? Would the loss of so many more B-29s have led to the deaths of U.S. Navy carrier airmen who in fact lived because the plane or bullet that might have shot them down was never created?

The argument will rage, as it has raged, unto the last breath of the last airman who landed at Iwo and the last relative of every Marine, soldier, or sailor who was martyred there. But who can say? There is no way for the calculus of war to achieve closure, nor for the calculus of life.

By war's end, the runways at Iwo had been completely hardtopped, and hardstands had been built for aircraft dispersal. By then, Marianas-based B-24 and B-29 groups shuttling to and from Japan had been routinely staging through Iwo for several months.
Official Signal Corps Photo

CHAPTER 17

D + 60 Years

In March 2005 a small flotilla of modern airliners assembled on Center Field, the last of Iwo's active runways. This was a one-day-a-year event. The only planes that fly to Iwo the rest of the year deliver supplies and rotate members of the four-hundred-man Japan Self-Defense Force garrison to and from the home islands. Once in a great while, modern U.S. Marines hold landing exercises on the island's hallowed beaches.

One way or another, the mainly Japanese and American visitors are pilgrims.

Two of the 2005 visitors are friends of mine. Colonel Dick Camp is a very old friend. He commanded an infantry company and was a general's aide in Vietnam. Lieutenant Colonel Dick Wilkerson, a new friend, was a radar-intercept officer in F-4 fighter-bombers in Vietnam. Both served full careers in the Marine Corps, and they share such an abiding love of Marine Corps history that they signed up for a transpacific historical tour so they could visit the battle sites—walk the ground—on which much of their training, all of their fidelity, and a huge amount of their spare time has been devoted to.

Among the pilgrims Camp and Wilkerson met were some "old guys" who had been there before, in February and March 1945. Though combat veterans themselves, the two younger career Marines stood in awe of the veterans, of whom few are left and fewer yet can make the arduous air journey.

In a very few years, there will be no veterans to remember those terrible and uplifting days.

At mean tide, the invasion beaches extend an average of 30 feet farther into the ocean than they did in 1945. This view is from just above Beach Blue, looking south toward Suribachi. Compare it with the many similar views in early chapters. *Compliments of Colonel Dick Camp*

This seemingly gentle rise is as difficult to ascend today as it was in early 1945. Dick Camp, who is still in terrific physical condition, was unable to "assault the high ground" from the surf line even though he was unencumbered by weapon, pack, and gear. Much younger men on the tour were likewise unable to bound forward at a steady jog. *Compliments of Colonel Dick Camp*

The landing beaches viewed from near the summit of Suribachi. The ribbon of road running diagonally from left to right across the bottom third of the photo was built by U.S. Navy Seabees while the battle to the north still raged—to service observation posts, radar stations, and other installations atop the volcano. *Compliments of Colonel Dick Camp*

The entire Japanese cave system is thought to be intact, though few visitors venture very far inside. There are no guides or maps available, and the handhewn caves through volcanic areas are disturbingly warm to within only a few yards of entrances. Note the effects of wind and weather, even on basaltic stones. *Compliments of Colonel Dick Camp*

A blown pillbox still stands silent sentry duty overlooking the invasion beaches. All such permanent defenses have been left in place. Indeed, isolated Iwo Jima might be one of the best-preserved battlefields on the planet. In sum, the defenses still impress visitors with the seriousness of the defenders' intent to kill all invaders. *Compliments of Colonel Dick Camp*

Suribachi from the air in March 2005. The vegetation that covers most of Iwo Jima today was planted in 1945 as a soil-conservation measure, but other types of flora have drifted in over the decades on ocean breezes and in bird droppings. *Compliments of Lieutenant Colonel Dick Wilkerson*

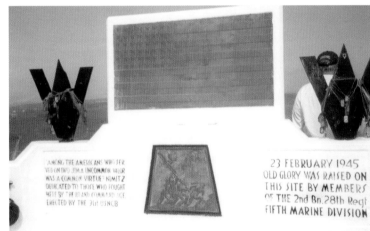

This memorial marks the spot of both flag raisings. The hundreds of dog tags that adorn the monument have been placed there as offerings of respect and fidelity by United States Marines who have visited the hallowed island during landing exercises or other postwar visits. *Compliments of Colonel Dick Camp*

Compliments of Lieutenant Colonel Dick Wilkerson

Bibliography

Bartley, Lieutenant Colonel Whitman S. *Iwo Jima: Amphibious Epic.* Washington, D.C.: Marine Corps Historical Branch, 1954.

Blakeney, Jane. *Heroes: U.S. Marine Corps, 1861–1955.* Blakeney Publishing, 1956.

Garand, George W., and Truman R. Strobridge. *Western Pacific Operations.* Vol. IV, *History of U.S. Marine Corps Operations in World War II.* Washington, D.C.: U.S. Marine Corps, 1971.

Hammel, Eric. *Air War Pacific: Chronology, America's Air War Against Japan in East Asia and the Pacific, 1941–1945.* Pacifica, Calif.: Pacifica Press, 1998.

———. *Pacific Warriors: The U.S. Marines in World War II, A Pictorial Tribute.* St. Paul, Minn.: Zenith Press, 2005.

Hammel, Eric, and John E. Lane. *Bloody Tarawa.* Pacifica, Calif.: Pacifica Press, 1998.

Hough, Frank O., Verle E. Ludwig, and Henry I. Shaw Jr. *Pearl Harbor to Guadalcanal.* Vol. I, *History of U.S. Marine Corps Operations in World War II.* Washington, D.C.: U.S. Marine Corps, 1958.

Mondey, David. *Concise Guide to American Aircraft of World War II.* London: Temple Press, 1982.

———. *Concise Guide to Axis Aircraft of World War II.* London: Temple Press, 1984.

Nalty, Bernard C. *The Right to Fight: African-American Marines in World War II.* Washington, D.C.: Marine Corps Historical Center, 1995.

Newcomb, Richard F. *Iwo Jima.* New York: Holt, Rinehart & Winston, 1965.

Olynyk, Frank J. *USMC Credits for the Destruction of Enemy Aircraft in Air-to-Air Combat, World War 2.* Aurora, Ohio: Frank J. Olynyk, 1981.

Ross, Bill D. *Iwo Jima: Legacy of Valor.* New York: Vanguard Press, 1985.

Sherrod, Robert. *History of Marine Corps Aviation in World War II.* San Rafael, Calif.: Presidio Press, 1980.

Toland, John. *The Rising Sun: The Decline and Fall of the Japanese Empire, 1936–1945.* New York: Random House, 1970.

Williams, Mary R. *Chronology: 1941–1945, U.S. Army in World War II.* Washington, D.C.: Center of Military History, 1984.

The author wholeheartedly recommends that readers interested in a full-blown narrative history of the Iwo Jima campaign read both Bill D. Ross's *Iwo Jima: Legacy of Valor* and Richard F. Newcomb's *Iwo Jima.* They are superb.

Index

United States Marine Corps Units index

2d 155mm Howitzer Battalion, 137

2d Armored Amphibian Battalion, 60

3d Marine Division, 47, 48, 129, 136, 162, 165, 166, 178, 181, 187, 188, 191, 197, 199, 200, 209, 212, 216, 217, 224, 225, 228

3d Medical Battalion, 162

3d Tank Battalion, 175, 183

4th Marine Division, 47–50, 60, 61, 63, 66, 70, 73, 80–82, 93–96, 129, 133, 134, 136, 139, 141, 143, 155, 159–161, 163, 169–171, 175, 181, 183, 184, 189, 196, 201, 202, 204, 212, 213, 216, 217, 220, 223, 224, 228

4th Tank Battalion, 77, 83, 97, 132, 134, 139, 175

5th Amphibian Truck Company, 62

V Amphibious Corps (VAC), 45, 47–50, 51, 72, 77, 93, 95, 127, 129, 135–137, 145, 156, 161, 165, 173, 180, 183, 187, 189, 190, 194, 196, 199–201, 207, 209, 212, 214, 217, 220, 222, 225

5th Engineer Battalion, 124, 127, 144

5th Marine Division, 47, 49, 50, 60–62, 69, 71, 74, 79, 85, 93, 105, 114, 127, 129, 130, 132, 135–137, 141, 146, 148, 149, 155, 156, 158, 163, 167, 169–171, 181, 183, 185, 186, 189, 196, 199, 201, 204, 209, 212, 216–218, 220, 225, 226, 228

5th Pioneer Battalion, Company C, 234

5th Tank Battalion, 75, 106, 124, 131, 159, 180, 186

5th Tank Battalion, Company C, 157

9th Marine Regiment (9th Marines), 165, 178, 181, 183, 189–191, 199, 214

1st Battalion (1/9)
Company B, 213

2d Battalion (2/9), 183, 192
Company E, 181, 182
Company G, 183

11th Amphibian Tractor Battalion
Company B, 96

12th Marine Regiment (12th Marines)
3d Battalion (3/12), 191

13th Marine Regiment (13th Marines), 62, 79
3d Battalion (3/13), 105, 112

14th Marine Regiment (14th Marines), 96, 159, 176
1st Battalion (1/14), 140
3d Battalion (3/14), 136
4th Battalion (4/14), 136, 137

21st Marine Regiment (21st Marines), 136, 141, 145, 154, 161, 162, 165, 180, 181, 190, 199, 209, 214, 225
1st Battalion (1/21), 148, 151, 154, 159
2d Battalion (2/21), 148, 151, 159
Company F, 16
3d Battalion (3/21), 174
Company L, 160, 174

23d Marine Regiment (23d Marines), 80, 134, 139, 142, 145, 148, 189, 196, 209, 214, 217, 225
1st Battalion (1/23), 60, 95, 132
Company B, 83
2d Battalion (2/23), 60, 69, 161
3d Battalion (3/23), 130, 190, 205

24th Marine Regiment (24th Marines), 133, 135, 136, 139, 154, 156, 181, 191, 201
1st Battalion (1/24), 80, 130, 135, 139, 140, 154
Company B, 136
2d Battalion (2/24), 130, 134, 145, 224

Company G, 139, 149
3d Battalion (3/24), 77, 80

25th Marine Regiment (25th Marines), 93, 95, 189, 196, 201, 209, 226
1st Battalion (1/25), 60, 72, 80, 130, 135–137, 140, 141, 154
Company A, 140
2d Battalion (2/25), 80, 130, 132, 135, 136, 141, 154, 156
3d Battalion (3/25), 60, 72, 77, 80, 83, 129, 130, 135, 139, 141, 151, 154, 156

26th Marine Regiment (26th Marines), 47, 48, 145, 154, 156, 181, 189, 228, 234
1st Battalion (1/26), 61, 130, 132, 145, 147, 155, 197, 204
Company C, 138
2d Battalion (2/26), 156, 207, 223
3d Battalion (3/26), 148, 157
Company F, 185
Company G, 148, 157
Company H, 196
Company I, 205

27th Marine Regiment (27th Marines), 47, 77, 132, 138, 145, 148, 189, 194, 196, 220, 225, 234
1st Battalion (1/27), 60, 132, 141, 216
2d Battalion (2/27), 60, 69, 132, 156
Company E, 215
Company F, 129
3d Battalion (3/27), 130, 132, 195
Company G, 193
Company H, 158
Weapons Company, 214

28th Marine Regiment (28th Marines), 47–49, 71, 95, 105, 106, 111–115, 123, 124, 126, 127, 199, 201, 228, 234
1st Battalion (1/28), 60,

67, 69, 74, 86, 105, 108, 111, 113, 115, 120, 126, 127, 129, 206
Company A, 81
Company B, 77
2d Battalion (2/28), 77, 222
Company D, 117
Company E, 110
3d Platoon, 117, 118
Company F, 115, 117
3d Battalion (3/28), 105, 106, 108, 113–115, 129, 208, 225

Fleet Marine Force, Pacific (FMFPac), 44, 48, 49, 51, 56, 129, 161, 197, 209

FMFPac Reconnaissance Battalion, 56

Marine Bombing Squadron (VMB)
VMB-612, 39, 40, 41, 244

Marine Fighting Squadron (VMF)
VMF-124, 42, 59
VMF-213, 42

Marine Observation Squadron (VMO)
VMO-1, 200
VMO-4, 165
VMO-5, 171

Marine Raider regiment, 48, 105, 117

Index of Equipment

A6M Zero fighter, 17, 18, 41, 42

B-24 Liberator heavy bomber, 20, 21, 25, 37, 39, 41, 43, 244, 247

B-25 Mitchell medium bomber, 26, 27

B-29 Superfortress very heavy bomber, 24, 25-27, 40, 41, 207–209, 212, 225, 235, 243–245, 247

C6N search plane, Nakajima, 40, 42

Dinah Might (B-29), 207–209

DUKW amphibian truck, 49, 62, 74, 94, 99, 136, 137

F4U Corsair fighter, 42, 61, 244

F6F Hellcat fighter, 17, 18

F6F-5 Hellcat, 18, 244

FM Wildcat ground-support fighter-bomber, 43, 165, 167

G4M medium bomber, 18, 40, 41

Landing craft, infantry, gunboat (LCI(G)), 54–56, 59, 204

Landing craft, infantry, rocket ship (LCI(R)), 54, 57, 105

Landing ship, medium (LSM), 51, 73–75, 95, 97

Landing ship, tank (LST), 51, 59, 62, 63, 86, 136, 144, 147, 168, 171

Landing craft, vehicle, personal (LCVP), 60, 61, 64, 65, 67, 75–77, 146

LVT(A)-4 armored amtrac, 59, 60, 69

M4 Sherman tank, 77, 83, 84, 97, 106, 124, 131, 132, 134, 135, 142, 145, 149, 157, 161, 173, 175, 180, 183, 185, 186, 192, 200, 218, 232

OA-10 Consolidated rescue seaplane, 245

OY observation plane, 165, 168, 171, 244

P-38 Lightning fighter, 26, 40, 41

P-47 Thunderbolt fighter, 21, 26, 40, 244

P-51 Mustang fighter, 26, 209, 212, 214, 217, 220, 235, 243, 244

P-61Black Widow fighter, 27

P-61 Northrup night fighter, 209, 212, 217, 235, 244

PB4Y Liberator heavy patrol bomber, 19, 39, 42, 209, 217

PB4Y-2 Privateer heavy patrol bomber, 244, 245

PBJ medium bomber, 37, 38, 244

PBM amphibious patrol bomber, 165, 167–169, 209

R4D transport, 201

SB2C Helldiver dive-bomber, 17, 18

TBM Avenger light bomber, 17, 18, 43, 171, 214, 217, 244

Type 97 medium tank, 36

Weasel tracked amphibian jeep, 97, 183

Weapons, 230–233

General Index

Allied Pacific War strategy, 23, 24
B-24 bombing campaign, 20, 21
Berry, Charles J., 204
Biak, Schouten Islands, 36
Bonin Islands, 17–19, 21, 26, 37, 40
Bougainville Island, 47, 48, 136, 160
Butt, Noah, 167
Caddy, William R., 205
Camp, Dick, 249, 250
Campbell, Robert, 120, 122
Casualties, 80, 243, 235
Cates, Clifton, 47, 48, 50, 161
Cave system, 30, 31, 33, 34, 250, 226
Center Airfield, 220, 225 see Motoyama Airfield No.2
Chambers, Justice M., 151, 154
Chichi Jima, 17–20, 30, 39, 42, 43, 169
Cole, Darrell S., 83
Craig, Edward, 48
Dunlap, Robert H., 138
East Boat Basin, 80, 129
Eniwetok Atoll, 18, 20
Erskine, Graves B., 47, 165, 166, 197
Fast Carrier Task Force, 23, 42
Flag raising, 117–127, 184, 222, 251
Gavutu Island, 141
Genaust, William, 119, 120, 122, 184
Gray, Ross F., 140
Guadalcanal Island, 40, 44, 48, 141, 142
Guam Island, 18, 23, 25, 27, 39, 47, 48, 120, 122, 136, 160, 165, 168, 169, 200, 209, 217, 243
Haha Jima, 17, 19, 39, 42, 235
Harrell, William G., 206
Hart, Franklin, 161
Herring, Rufus G., 56
Higashi Rock, 53
Hill 362-A, 194, 195, 199
Hill 382, 36, 183, 184, 196, 199, 201
Hill 383, 189
Honshu Island, Japan, 43
Imperial Japanese Army, 33, 36, 41
    2d Independent Mixed Brigade, 30
    109th Infantry Division, 30
    145th Infantry Regiment, 30, 159

Imperial Japanese Navy, 18, 21, 33, 40, 42, 169, 171, 235
Iwo Jima Air Support Plan, 42
Jacobson, Douglas T., 190
Japan Self-Defense Force, 249
Johnson, Chandler, 117, 118, 120, 201
Joint Assault Signal Company (JASCO), 49, 213
Julian, Joseph R., 216
Kitano Point, 225
Kobe, Japan, 26
Kuribayashi, Tadamichi, 29, 30, 36, 37, 56, 74, 93, 108, 159, 163, 177, 178, 226
Kwajalein Atoll, 47, 48
LaBelle, James D., 214
Landing Beaches
    Blue, 95, 249
    Blue-1, 47, 72, 80, 103
    Green, 47, 67, 69, 71, 77, 86, 105
    Purple, 169
    Red, 95, 96
    Red-1, 47, 69
    Red-2, 47, 69
    Yellow, 44, 91, 95, 143
    Yellow-1, 47, 136
    Yellow-2, 47, 69, 133, 134
Leatherneck magazine, 118
Leims, John H., 213
Lindbergh, Charles A., 25
Liversedge, Harry, 48
Lowery, Lou, 118
Lucas, Jacklyn H., 132
Lummus, Jack, 215
Makin Raid, 48
Malo, R. Fred, 207
Mariana Islands, 17, 19, 23–27, 42–47, 199, 201, 202, 220, 225, 243, 247
Marshall Islands, 62
Martin, Harry L., 234
McCarthy, Joseph J., 139
Medal of Honor, 56, 81, 83, 110, 132, 138–140, 151, 154, 190, 192, 193, 195, 204–208, 213–216, 222–224, 234
Minami, 189, 201, 204, 209
Motoyama Airfield No. 1, 17, 21, 80, 82, 129, 130, 133–136, 141, 155, 161, 162, 165–169, 178, 189, 201–203, 207, 209, 217
Motoyama Airfield No.2, 17, 47, 129, 138, 141, 142, 145, 148, 149, 151, 156–162,

165, 174, 178, 180, 181, 189, 191–193, 199
Motoyama Airfield No. 3, 190, 196, 200
Mount Suribachi, 17, 21, 35, 43, 47, 53, 59, 71, 77, 105–115, 120, 122–127, 129, 184, 196, 249, 250, 251
Navy Cross, 119
New Georgia Island invasion, 44
New Guinea, 36
Nishi Ridge, 201
Nishi village, 196
North Airfield, 220, 235 see Motoyama Airfield No.3
O-1 objective line, 47, 132, 138, 145, 156, 180
O-2 objective line, 156, 162, 180, 190
O-3 objective line, 190, 214
O-A objective line, 180, 183
Okinawa Island, 171, 200, 212
Operation DETACHMENT, 47, 48
Pacific Fleet amphibious force, 101
Pacific Theater intelligence commmand, 49
Peatross, Oscar, 48
Peleliu Island, 36, 120
Philippine Islands, 24, 43
Phillips, George, 222
Pollack, Alfred, 48
Radio Tokyo, 56
Rock Quarry, 72, 80, 140
Rockey, Keller E., 47, 146
Rosenthal, Joe, 120, 122, 124
Ruhl, Donald J., 110
Saipan Island, 17–21, 23, 25, 30, 40, 41, 47, 48, 54, 101, 119, 243
Schmidt, Harry, 45, 48, 57, 136, 161, 162, 165
Schrier, Harold George, 117, 118, 124
Seabees, 165, 167, 220, 235, 250
Sigler, Franklin E., 223
Silver Star, 151
Smith, Holland M., 44–45, 48, 57, 161, 197
Solomon Islands, 24, 47, 48
South Airfield, 220 see Motoyama Airfield No. 1
Spruance, Raymond, 45, 57
Stein, Tony, 81
Tachiiwa Point, 217
Tarawa Atoll, 44, 101
Tinian Island, 23, 25, 41, 47, 209, 243

Tojo, Hideki, 29
Truk Atoll, 24
Tulagi Island, 151
Turner, Richmond Kelly, 44, 45, 51, 57, 197, 217
United States Army, 23, 36, 49
    147th Infantry Regiment, 228
United States Army Air Forces, 20, 21, 26, 27, 40, 42, 169, 209, 212, 214, 217, 220, 244, 245, 247
    VII Bomber Command, 41, 42, 43
    VII Fighter Command, 25, 41, 209, 212, 217, 220, 235, 243, 244
    9th Very Heavy Bombardment Group, 207
    XXI Bomber Command, 26, 40, 42, 183
21st Fighter Group, 235
United States Coast Guard, 78
United States Navy, 17, 24, 18–20, 27, 33, 37, 39, 40, 42, 50, 59, 78, 142, 167–169, 201, 217, 247, 250
    9th Naval Construction Brigade, 155 see Seabees
    Amphibious Support Carrier Group, 42
    Fifth Fleet, 45, 59, 93, 212
    LCI(G) 449, 56
    LCI(G) Group 8, 56
    LST 779, 12
    Task Force 38, 21, 42
    Task Force 53, 59
    Task Force 58, 43, 43, 45, 51, 59 155, 183
    Task Group 38.4, 21
    Task Group 52.2, 43, 212
    Task Group 58.1, 17, 18, 20
    Task Group 58.3, 20
    Task Group 58.4, 17
    Underwater demolition team (UDT), 45, 53, 54
    USS Anzio, 169, 171, 212
    USS Arkansas, 43
    USS Bismarck Sea, 144, 214
    USS Essex, 42, 59
    USS Lunga Point, 144
    USS Missoula, 117
    USS Nevada, 55
    USS Pensacola, 53, 54
    USS Samaritan, 120
    USS Saratoga, 142
    USS Spearfish, 59
    USS Tennessee, 53

Ulithi Atoll, 200, 214, 217
Volcano Islands, 17–19, 21, 26, 39, 40
Wahlen, George E., 207
Walsh, William C., 193
Watson, Wilson D., 192
Wilkerson, Dick, 249
Williams, Hershel W., 154
Williams, Jack, 208
Williams, Robert, 48
Willis, John H., 195
World War I, 48

Official USMC Photo